CRASH COURSE

ACHIEVING PHYSICAL & FINANCIAL RECOVERY AFTER AN ACCIDENT

SIXTH EDITION

JOHN M. GRAHAM, ATTORNEY AT LAW

of

GRAHAM LUNDBERG & PESCHEL

Injury Attorneys since 1979

(800) 422–4610   North Puget Sound
(800) 273–5005   South Puget Sound

LEGAL EDUCATIONAL PRESS

GLPattorneys.com

CRASH COURSE 101

A Legal Educational Press Book

Publishing History
trade paperback 1st edition / August 1995
trade paperback 2nd edition / March 1996
trade paperback 3rd edition / October 1999
trade paperback 4th edition / February 2005
trade paperback 5th edition / April 2010
trade paperback 6th edition / April 2011

Library of Congress Catalog Card Number: 94-12045

The reader is notified that this text is an educational tool, not a practice book.
Since the law is in constant flux, no rule or statement of law in this book should be
relied upon. The reader should always refer to standard legal sources for current rule
or law. If legal advice is required, the services of an attorney should be sought.

For information:
Legal Educational Press
P.O. Box 2428
Kirkland, WA 98083
Tel: (425) 827–1111
CRASHCOURSE101.COM

ISBN 0–9644750–5–7

Legal Educational Press & logo are registered
in the U.S. Patent and Trademark Office.

Introduction

YOU'RE PROBABLY READING THIS GUIDEBOOK
because you've recently experienced an automobile collision.
After surviving you are faced with some disturbing difficulties.
You're suddenly without a car and you've been injured. The
tasks of managing your care can be overwhelming. Inability
to work means no paychecks coming in. Your money woes are
mounting. In addition, the claims process is a complicated one.
You will need to learn a new language and hire experts to be
on your team.

After a collision causing injury, wouldn't it be great to have a
road map? At this time you need step-by-step legal assistance
that will help you understand your case, the questions to ask
and whether you are getting correct answers.

Over the years, I've discovered that everyone making an
insurance claim needs guidance. This book will assist in
determining whether you need an attorney, the best ways to
hire one and how to work effectively with him. Our law offices,
GRAHAM LUNDBERG & PESCHEL, have helped many people
in Washington State reduce the stress of making their injury
claim and achieve full recovery after an automobile collision.
When writing Crash Course 101, my aim was to combine
30+ years of professional experiences with my strong personal
commitment to full physical and financial recovery in an easy
to read, understandable and helpful guidebook.

Crash Course 101 provides the information and the tools needed to effectively and efficiently participate more fully in your own insurance claim.

Many of the strategies that I've learned over the years are contained in this book. If you think you need help beyond what is offered here, give us a call. I've assembled one of the largest and best personal injury teams in Washington, with multiple offices throughout the entire state. Our goal, both in this book and in our professional practice at GLP is to provide you with the best possible legal service.

Our toll-free number is (800) 422-4610 for the entire state of Washington.

You can reach us on the internet at GLPattorneys.com.

Schedule a free consultation at one of our local neighborhood offices nearest you, and we will answer any questions you may have about your case. The first question should be: "Do I need an attorney?"

If you're stranded at the crossroads of confusion following an automobile collision, Crash Course 101 will teach you what you need to know to get back on the road to full recovery. This book puts you back in the driver's seat.

Your journey begins here. May it lead to a full and successful recovery!

TABLE OF CONTENTS

Chapter 1 Property Damage   1

Towing   2

Storage   4

Automobile Repairs   6

Pocketing the Money   8

Payment for Repair Charges   8

Taking Delivery of Your Repaired Car   9

Repair of Personal Items   10

Rental Car   11

Total Loss   12

Diminution in Value   14

Document Everything!   15

Summary   17

  Survival Guide Checklist   19

Chapter 2 Understanding Insurance Coverages   21

Asking the Right Questions   22

Identifying Available Insurance Policies   24

Determining Coverage for Injuries   31

Stacking Insurance Policies   32

When the Insurance Company is Slow to Pay   33

Determining Liability   34

Negotiating with the Key Players   35

Insurance Reimbursement   36

Bill Submission and Payment   38

Summary   40

  Survival Guide Checklist   41

Chapter 3   Personal Injury Protection (PIP)   43

What is PIP?   44

Why PIP?   44

How Much Does PIP Pay?   46

PIP and Your Insurance Company   48

How Do I Claim My PIP Benefits?   51

Plan Ahead!   53

Summary   54

   Survival Guide Checklist   55

Chapter 4   The Perils of Handling Your Own Claim   57

Should I Represent Myself?   58

The Three Major Qualifiers   59

   Time   60

   Temperament   64

   Talent   67

How Does the System Treat Pro Se Claimants?   69

When Do I Need an Attorney?   72

How Can an Attorney Help Me?   78

Summary   82

   Survival Guide Checklist   83

Chapter 5   Finding the Right Attorney   85

What is a Personal Injury Attorney?   86

Finding a Good Referral   86

Your First Phone Call   88

Warning Signs!	90
The Initial Consultation	90
Assessing the Initial Interview	92
That Old Familiar Feeling	93
Qualifying an Injury Attorney to Handle Your Case	95
When You Meet With an Attorney	96
Clarify Your Expectations	99
Fees and Costs	99
Fee Agreement	100
Contractual Obligations	100
Contingency Fee	101
Costs	103
Communications	106
Summary	107
Survival Guide Checklist	109

Chapter 6 Managing Your Medical Care   111

Making Your Way Through the Medical Maze	112
Follow-up Care	113
What if I'm Not Recovering?	114
Don't Shop Until You Drop!	116
Managing Your Recovery	117
Communicating with Your Medical Caregivers	118
Managing Your Medical Records	120
Involving the Whole Medical Team	121
Managing Multiple Caregivers	122

TABLE OF CONTENTS

Traditional vs. Alternative Medical Care   124

Chiropractic   124

Holistic Alternatives   126

Maximum Medical Improvement (MMI)   127

Being the Good Patient   130

Summary   132

     Survival Guide Checklist   133

Chapter 7   Proving Longlasting Impacts From an Accident   135

The True Impact of an Automobile Collision   136

Physical Injuries   137

Injuries to the Head and Brain   138

The Other Side of Physical Injury: Depression   140

     Depression Checklist   142

Documenting the Effects of the Collision on Your Employment   144

Proving Wage Loss   147

     Wage Loss Checklist   147

Documenting How the Injury Affects Your Ability to Work   148

     Quality of Work Checklist   151

Documenting How Your Injury Affects Your Quality of Life   152

     Quality of Life Checklist   153

Summary   157

     Survival Guide Checklist   159

Chapter 8 Strategies Attorneys Use To Resolve Cases   161
           Marshaling Records and Bills   162
           Determining the Value of Your Case   164
           Legal Negotiation Strategies   168
           Building an Effective Demand Package   175
           Arbitration   178
           Mediation   180
           Litigation   183
           Summary   187
                Survival Guide Checklist   189

           Index   191
           Acronyms   203
           About Graham Lundberg & Peschel   204
           About the Author   206

PROPERTY DAMAGE

*I*f you've been in an automobile collision, count yourself lucky if the only thing damaged was your car. Personal injuries caused by an automobile collision are traumatic, painful and often expensive to treat and heal. Damage to your automobile can also be traumatic, painful and expensive to fix! If your car was damaged in a collision, you'll find helpful information in this chapter about your rights and obligations when seeking repairs.

Remember, if you've been injured in a collision, your first priority on your road to physical recovery is to get immediate competent medical care. But don't overlook the importance of pursuing and getting maximum reimbursement for damages to your car promptly after the collision. Let's take a look at some of the facts and fiction about what you should and shouldn't do when it comes to getting your damaged car repaired at the insurance company's expense.

Towing

Who pays when your car needs to be towed after being damaged in a collision by a negligent driver? If you were injured in the collision and incapable of driving your car away from the scene, it was probably towed to the nearest wrecking yard. Perhaps your car was so heavily damaged that it was rendered inoperable. In either case, you are faced with what can become sizable charges for towing and storage. Let's talk about who is responsible for paying for what, and how you go about making sure that you are reimbursed for any towing and storage expenses.

The party that eventually ends up paying depends on proving who was at fault in the collision. If a party breaches any legal duty, that party may be "liable." In this book, we are going to assume that you were the damaged party and that the other driver was at fault and is responsible for your losses. Unfortunately, many auto collisions are caused by actions and circumstances that can lead to frustrating, protracted battles over proving who's at fault. Sometimes these cases become complex early on. When that happens, the likelihood of your obtaining a speedy reimbursement for your out-of-pocket towing and storage expenses from the other party's insurance carrier diminishes as the duration of the battle lengthens.

Sometimes, your car will be towed more than once, from the scene of the collision to a wrecking yard, and then from the wrecking yard to a body shop. Towing charges add up, and if your car sits in the wrecking yard for any period of time, storage charges will also grow as each day ticks by.

You may be reimbursed by several sources, including your own insurance company, the negligent party's insurance company, or the negligent party.

If your car is towed, you are responsible for the towing bill. The towing company that takes your car from the scene of the collision will look to you for payment. When you go to the storage yard to retrieve your car, you will be asked to pay all the charges in full, and usually in cash, before your car is released. You must then look to your insurance company or the negligent driver's insurance company for reimbursement. If the negligent driver does not have insurance, he will be individually responsible for your reimbursement.

If you are injured in the collision and are unable to drive, or if your car cannot be driven because of extensive damage, your insurance company will often arrange to have your car towed to a repair shop. The repair shop will then add that towing bill to your repair bill, and it will become part of the charges reimbursed by the insurance company after your car is repaired.

In a perfect world, the other driver would be clearly negligent and have insurance, and you also would have insurance. In this situation, you have the choice of requesting either your insurance company or the negligent driver's insurance company reimburse you for all out-of-pocket towing and storage expenses.

If there is some debate as to negligence and liability, you may be cooling your heels for a long time as the various parties sort through the facts of the collision. If this is the case, you should immediately request that your insurance company pay for towing, storage and rental car expenses. You don't want to wait for a determination of liability while the storage fees add up and you are left without transportation.

Call your insurance company and make a collision report. Ask the important questions: Do I have rental car reimbursement? Do I have collision coverage? Even if I'm at fault, am I covered? Will I be reimbursed for towing charges? If you have adequate coverage, your agent will begin the process of protecting you and providing reimbursement for your losses.

If you don't have adequate coverage, you'll unfortunately find out why you should have had it. While the other driver's insurance company is taking time to evaluate the collision and make a determination of liability, you will be left holding what can turn out to be a very costly bag of costs and expenses that would have been easily handled by your insurance company if you had obtained adequate coverage in the first place.

Washington law requires all drivers to carry a minimum amount of automobile insurance. After a collision, you will likely deal with two insurance companies, yours, and that of the negligent driver. Often, one of the insurance companies will want to have your car towed from the storage facility to its own appraisal facility or to a repair shop of its choice to examine and evaluate the damage to your car. The negligent driver is responsible for towing charges incurred by the insurance company to conduct a damage appraisal.

Storage

Once your car has been towed to a storage facility, daily charges begin to add up. The negligent driver is responsible for reimbursing you for all storage charges, from the time of the collision to the time the insurance company authorizes release of your car for repairs.

The insurance company is obligated to act in "good faith." In the State of Washington, "bad faith" is the absence of good faith. It doesn't necessarily mean that the insurance company has to show ill will, or a determined effort to make your life miserable, as you attempt to settle the claim. It does mean that the insurance company, and its employees and agents, must work with due diligence to settle your claim responsibly and expeditiously. They must provide a fair market value replacement for all of your losses to make you "whole" again, that is, as you were before the collision.

> If you postpone repair of your car because of a dispute with the insurance company, you may be held personally liable for any storage expenses incurred. The law requires you to reasonably mitigate, or lessen, your own damages. You can't abandon your car for three months at the storage yard and expect the insurance company to compensate you for the charges.

You have the right to remove personal belongings from your car, upon showing proof that you own the car. Sometimes you will be granted ready access to your car accompanied by watchful storage facility employees. They share your concern that valuable items may be removed from your car by unauthorized persons while it is stored on their property.

When you are granted access to your car by the storage facility, it is important that you obtain an accurate, detailed receipt for every item you remove from your car.

Let's say that the storage yard was cooperative and let you remove your brand new stereo speakers from your car before your car was towed to the repair shop. Later you are shocked to discover that your valuable seat covers are missing. Without a detailed receipt from the storage yard clearly stating that all you removed was the stereo speakers, you are going to have a hard time proving that you did not also take the seat covers when you were given access to your car.

Sometimes you will be refused access to your car because the facility does not want to assume responsibility for what may happen to your car and to the items and equipment in it. It can be frustrating facing off with a wrecking yard "go-fer" who, with greasy arms firmly crossed, obstinately refuses to allow you to retrieve valuable business papers from your car.

> While your car is in storage, daily charges are accumulating. It is important that you or your representative contact the negligent driver's insurance company immediately to make arrangements for the repair of your car. The insurance adjuster is obligated to act in good faith to expeditiously process the towing and repair of your car. It is to your advantage to actively negotiate with the insurance companies, and therefore reduce added storage charges you will be obligated to pay up front.

What can you do? Unfortunately, the law is not clear on this issue. Sometimes nothing short of your paying to have your car towed off of their "protected" property and to the repair shop will provide access to your own car. Call the insurance agent handling your claim and request assistance in gaining access to your car.

Automobile Repairs

You have the right to have your car repaired by any body shop you choose. Insurance companies typically avoid any semblance of an affiliation with any one body shop, to avoid being in an uncomfortable position if you discover later that the repairs were inadequate or defective.

Everyone has stories about the "Body Shop Nightmare." If you do not already know of a reputable body shop, check around. Ask your family, friends and co-workers. Call your own insurance agent for a recommendation. Call the Better Business Bureau and ask about the reputation of local shops.

Have the insurance company deal directly with the repair shop. This provides an 'implied warranty' that the insurance company will back up the body shop and help guarantee the work.

Once your car has been delivered to the body shop, you can begin negotiating with the negligent driver's insurance company to decide which insurance company pays for the repairs to your car. If you decide to have your insurance company pay, they will send an adjuster to the repair shop. The adjuster and the repair shop will negotiate appropriate repairs and costs. They compare their evaluations of the damage and refer to automobile repair guidelines that provide the prevailing rates. The adjuster and the repair shop agree to the appraised charges, and the work is performed on your car.

Your insurance company cuts a check directly to the repair shop for the work and for any towing expenses that were "fronted" by the repair shop. Your insurance company will then request and obtain reimbursement from the negligent driver or their insurance company for the cost of repairs to your car.

If you request that the negligent driver's insurance company cover the cost of repairs, they will work with the repair shop to determine a fair repair cost. They will pay the repair shop directly for the repairs to your car.

Pocketing the Money

In the alternative, you can take your car to several different body shops for estimates. You can submit all of the estimates, or only the highest ones, to the insurance company. They will review the estimates and negotiate with you on the amount of money they will pay for repairs. They will probably send their adjuster out to look at your car and provide their own in-house estimate. When the insurance company writes you the check, you can take your car and the money to the body shop of your choice and have the repairs completed. Or, you can pocket the money and not repair your car at all.

The disadvantage of pocketing the money is that it represents a release by you. You are in essence saying that you've settled your claim for property damage. You are out of luck if you later discover that there is additional, more costly damage to your car that was not included in the settlement. Don't try to work a deal where you pocket the money and repair the car yourself, or have your favorite uncle repair it, or worse yet, not repair it at all. It is to your advantage to have it repaired by a reputable body shop that will perform quality work.

Payment for Repair Charges

The body shop will often coordinate other repairs to your car that cannot be made at their facility. If the upholstery has to be cleaned, or the windshield needs replacing, the body shop will coordinate with other businesses to provide these services. They will add their charges to the body shop bill and submit all charges to the insurance company for payment.

The body shop will use new factory parts if your car is less than three years old. After three years, used parts are customarily used. You may request that only new, "OEM" parts be used to repair your car if it is more than three years old. However, you will pay the cost difference between a used part and a new one.

All of the charges submitted to the insurance company must be for repair of collision related damage. The insurance adjuster must be satisfied that the repairs are legitimate before paying for the charges.

The "life expectancy" of your car's parts are also factored into the amount of money the insurance company is willing to pay for repairs. For example, if your tires have 20,000 miles of wear, they have already "used up" 50% of their 40,000 mile life expectancy. If they were destroyed in the collision, the insurance company will reimburse you 50% of the tires' life expectancy. The same rule holds for mufflers, brakes and other parts that customarily wear out over time.

The body shop will typically repaint only those sections of the car that suffered damage. If your car is more than a few years old, you will probably be able to see a difference between new and original paint. Again, you can request that the entire car be repainted, but you will pay the difference between painting the damaged sections and painting the whole car. The insurance company is not obligated to pay for repainting undamaged sections of your car.

Taking Delivery of Your Repaired Car

Washington State law requires that your car be in the same condition after repair as it was before the collision. If you find that you car is not in the same condition, it will be a bone of contention between you and the paying insurance company. Once the repairs are completed, it is important that you perform a complete examination and evaluation of your car before accepting delivery of the car.

If you feel that the car is not properly aligned or that things "just aren't right," the insurance company will insist that unibody cars are repaired to factory precision and that your car has been returned to its condition prior to the accident. You have the right hire a professional automobile appraiser, at your expense, to evaluate and document the condition of your car following repair. This objective evaluation may be worth the expense if you are disputing the repairs with the insurance company and the body shop.

It's difficult and sometimes impossible to prove six months down the line that your car's brakes are failing because of damage incurred during the collision or that your trunk leaks a year later because the seals were broken upon impact. The insurance company will look closely at all opportunities you may have had to discover the problem earlier. Also, it will be your duty to prove to the insurance company or to a court that the cause of the problem was the collision itself. Normal wear and tear, or a pre-existing condition, or another subsequent collision will quickly reduce your claim for additional damage.

Repair of Personal Items

You are entitled to retrieve and repair or replace items of personal property that were damaged in the collision. Perhaps your set of golf clubs in the trunk was crushed on impact or the leather jacket you were wearing was ripped when you struck the steering wheel. The insurance company will want to see proof of the value of these items, such as a bill of sale. If you do not have that, photographs of the items prior to the collision would be helpful. With or without reliable documentation, submit a claim for losses of personal items. Negotiate with the insurance company for satisfactory reimbursement for repairs or for the replacement value of the items.

Rental Car

You should never lie about age, insurance or any other fact on the rental contract. Fraudulent information will void any insurance coverage provided under the contract if you get in a collision in the rental car.

When your car is damaged and you lose the use of your car, you are entitled by law to a replacement vehicle. The negligent driver is required to either rent a car for you, or pay you for loss of use of your car during the period that your car is disabled. The replacement car does not have to equal your car in value or quality. So, if your brand new Cadillac is sitting in the repair shop awaiting repair, the rental car provided by the insurance company may very well be an economy compact. Typically, you will be reimbursed $20.00 per day for a rental car for the time between when your car was damaged in the collision, and when your car is repaired and returned to its prior condition. You may upgrade your rental car from the model offered at the $20.00 insurance rate, but you are responsible for any increased charges due to the upgrade.

You are required to show proof of automobile insurance when you sign the rental contract. Many rental companies will not rent to individuals under the age of 25. Also, many rental companies will demand payment by way of a credit card. The insurance company is not obligated to provide a rental car if you do not meet the rental contract requirements.

If you do not meet the requirements of the rental agency providing the rental car, you may have someone else rent the car for you and name you on the contract as an authorized driver. Failing that, you may have no choice but to accept the $20 per day payment from the insurance company and to rely on the good graces of friendly drivers, the bus or your own two feet to get where you need to go.

Many body shops provide rental cars on the premises. When you drop your car off for repair, you can get a rental car right there. When you return to the shop to drop off the rental car and pick up your repaired car, the repair shop will simply add the rental charges onto your bill, and the insurance company will write a check for the full amount.

You may not need a rental car while your damaged car is in for repairs. Perhaps you have a second car or maybe your injuries preclude you from driving while your car is being repaired. You are nevertheless entitled to reimbursement of $20.00 per day during the period that you are without your car. If the insurance company doesn't offer you the reimbursement, speak up and ask for it!

Total Loss

The determination of "total loss" of your car is far from an exact science. A typical approach is the "70% rule." If your car suffers damages totaling 70% of its value, the insurance company will likely write your car off as a total loss and issue you a check that represents the fair market value of your car before the collision. You sign the car over to the insurance company, which in turn sells it to a salvage yard.

Do you have the right to demand that your car be repaired? Washington law says that the negligent party has to pay to repair the car, or reimburse you the fair market value of the car, whichever is less. The law doesn't address the total loss of a car. If your car is worth $10,000, and there is $7,000 worth of damage, the negligent driver has to pay you $7,000 to get your car repaired.

If the insurance company declares your car a total loss, and you still want to keep your car, you can make an offer to the insurance company. Perhaps you would like to cannibalize the car for parts, or attempt to repair the car yourself. You can do that, but you end up effectively "buying" your car from the insurance company. The insurance company will sell you your car for the same price that a salvage yard bids to purchase the wreck. You do have the option of obtaining bids from salvage yards to assist you in negotiating with the insurance company for a fair "purchase price" of the totaled car.

If your car is deemed a total loss, the car's title is changed to reflect that. This is done to protect subsequent purchasers of your car by alerting them to its history of substantial damages.

Let's say your car is valued at $10,000, and the salvage yard offers $3,000 for the wreck. If you opt to "buy" your car from the insurance company, they will give you $10,000 minus the $3,000, for a total of $7,000. After you receive your $7,000, you are responsible for towing the car to your chosen destination, paying any storage costs and repairing or disposing of the car.

The no hassle approach, of course, is to accept a check for $10,000 from the insurance company, turn the car over to them, cash the check and go buy yourself a replacement car.

Diminution in Value

Washington law says that the negligent driver has to pay for the diminution, or decrease, in value to your car, even though it has been repaired. You've paid $3,000 for repairs to your car, and now the car is worth less than it was before, because it was damaged in the collision.

The insurance company will refer to any one of a number of "Blue Books" to determine an appropriate valuation for your car. Keep in mind that insurance adjusters will generally select the lowest valuation for your car. They will refer to the listing for the same make, model, year and mileage as your car and offer you a "fair market value" based on the listed information.

How do you go about proving that there has been a diminution, or reduction, in the value of your car? There are two primary determinations to be made: the value of your car immediately before the accident, and the value of your car immediately after repairs.

How do you prove the value of your car before the collision? If you are one of the rare people who has a long history of repairs by one reputable shop, you can have them examine your car and attest to its condition prior to the collision. Most repair shops are not enthusiastic about doing this, because it's difficult to accurately assess the exact condition of a car just prior to the moment of impact in a collision.

If you can afford to, you can hire an independent appraiser to evaluate your car and provide a fair market value. The appraiser will examine your car, evaluate the present market, look at comparable sales, and most importantly, determine the value of your car before the collision. Many insurance companies use independent appraisers in their own valuations, and an appraiser's report could provide helpful to your case.

Document Everything!

Your negotiations will be more effective when you can produce recent repair bills, photographs of your car and letters and documentation from auto dealers attesting to the market value of your car or similar cars of like make, model, mileage and condition. Look in recent issues of the Auto Trader and other regional automobile classified ads for comparisons and valuations of cars like yours. You will need to determine the asking price, and most importantly, the selling price. Call some of the people who have advertised a car like yours and ask them how much they got for the car.

Write down all the information you gather, make photocopies, collect every document you can get your hands on and take your case to the insurance adjuster. You'll often find that when presented with convincing documentation, insurance adjusters are willing to re-evaluate their first offer and come up with a figure that may be more acceptable to you. The adjuster wants to settle your claim as quickly as possible for the least amount of money. When you do the legwork for the adjuster and provide convincing documentation that shows a higher valuation for your car, chances are you'll receive a higher payment. It's definitely worth the time and effort to negotiate with documentation in hand if you encounter an unsatisfactory first offer from the adjuster.

Will you ever get "full value" for your damaged car? Not likely. If you just bought a brand new car, drove it off the lot and got creamed at the next intersection, it is highly unlikely that you will receive the full amount of money that you paid the dealer just moments before the collision. Your car depreciated dramatically in value from the moment you first started the engine and drove it off the dealer's lot. Most of us pay an inflated price for the cars we buy from a dealer. That's the nature of the car business. The insurance company is not about to accept your arguments that what you paid for the car is equal to the actual fair market value of the car. You may have paid $18,000 for that sporty little beauty, but the insurance company will counter with a $14,000 fair market valuation. You probably won't be able to boost that seemingly low valuation any higher.

What if you don't agree with the insurance company's valuation? You can negotiate. When your car is damaged in a collision, there are two important things to do when negotiating with the insurance company: negotiate in person and provide ample documentation.

Summary

After an automobile collision, attending to the repair or replacement of your car often seems like the most important thing you need to do. It's amazing how quickly we feel helpless and stranded without our trusted car in one piece and parked conveniently in the garage! In this chapter, we covered what you need to do immediately after an automobile collision to ensure that your car and your personal possessions are returned to you, or replaced, so that you are in the same condition after the collision as you were before.

The most important thing you need to remember, and the most important job you need to accomplish after an automobile collision, is devoting all of your energies to full physical recovery. While it may seem that the only thing you really want and need right now is to get your car back, return to work, and get your life back on track, none of these things are going to be possible or even of any use to you if you do not have the good health and physical ability to enjoy them.

If you've been injured in an automobile collision, wait until you've sufficiently recovered before you attempt to solve all of the hassles involved in getting your car repaired or replaced. The better alternative is to hire a competent personal injury attorney immediately. Let his or her team begin as early as possible working on your case. Let them investigate the accident, take photos of the accident scene, damaged cars, collect witness statements and contact insurance companies. Now that you know what needs to be done to obtain full compensation for damages to your car, you, or a trusted family member or friend who steps in on your behalf, can ensure that the damages to your car are satisfactorily handled by your insurance company. If injured, hire an attorney to represent you and handle all of the details of your claim.

Whomever you choose to oversee the repair or replacement
of your car, nothing is more important than your physical
recovery. Your car and your other material possessions are
replaceable. That's why you have automobile insurance!
Your health and well-being, on the other hand, are far more
fragile and can't be replaced with a check from the insurance
company. Physical recovery demands a great degree of vigilant
care on your part. That's why we'll be talking a little later in
this book about maximizing your physical recovery. Hiring
an attorney immediately will reduce your stress, minimize
your anxiety and allow you to better focus on your physical
recovery.

Survival Guide *Checklist*

✓	Property Damage
	Your physical recovery should be your top priority!
	Get your car out of storage immediately. Insurance companies do not reimburse for these costs.
	Work with the system to get your car repaired correctly the first time.
	Document! Document!! Document!!!
	Take digital photos of all damaged cars, yours and theirs, and the accident scene.
	Understand the terms total loss and market value.
	Negotiate in person.
	Know your consumer rights.
	If injured, immediately find and hire the best personal injury attorney.

UNDERSTANDING INSURANCE COVERAGES

*W*hen was the last time you asked yourself, "What insurance do I have?" Better yet, when was the last time you were able to answer that question? Unfortunately, too often folks find that they know little or nothing about the policies they've purchased to insure their health, automobiles, homes, businesses and even their credit cards, in the event of loss, damage or injury.

Now that you need to use that automobile insurance policy, do you even know what it does and doesn't cover? If you're like most people, you probably don't. Most of us buy insurance because we know it's the right and prudent thing to do. We depend on our agent to make many of our choices, hopefully in our best interest. But when the time comes to make a claim against a policy, or multiple policies, too often we find ourselves asking all the questions then that we should have asked when we first signed on the dotted line.

Asking the Right Questions

This chapter will give you the information you need to investigate all of your insurance options, and equip you with the knowledge and facts that you need to claim all of the benefits to which you are legally entitled. You'll learn how to:

- Identify all available insurance payment sources.
- Know what to look for in an insurance policy.
- Submit your bills to the appropriate insurer.
- Pursue full payment of your claims.

Am I covered for all collisions? What if I'm physically injured? What if the collision was my fault? And what about towing? What if I'm unable to work because of my injuries? How am I going to pay my personal bills and the mortgage? How much will the policy pay? Can my insurance company refuse to pay for medical care? How long will payments continue after the collision? Whom should I turn to for payment, my own insurance policy (first-party insurance) or the other driver's policy (third-party insurance)?

What is "full coverage"? If you have liability, uninsured and underinsured motorist coverage, collision, comprehensive, towing, rental car and PIP coverage, you are probably adequately covered. Review your policy yearly to make sure the policy limits are adequate and appropriate. The answers to these questions about coverage and limits are always determined by:

- The actual language in the policy.
- Whether the policy was in force at the time of the collision.

- ◆ The case law (previous legal rulings that have been made in similar situations).
- ◆ Other statutes and laws.
- ◆ The facts of the collision.

> An attorney should provide a preliminary review of your case at no cost. He or she will advise you of the merits of your claim, and whether he can help you or if you can easily settle the claim on your own. Call an attorney specializing in personal injury, and ask if an initial consultation is free. Those free 60 minutes could determine the difference between $500 in your pocket and $5,000.

Some of your questions can bring surprising answers. Maybe you've gotten lucky and your insurance agent has provided thorough coverage. Take the time after an accident to understand the policy coverages to maximize your benefits.

On the other hand, if you have inadequate or nonexistent insurance coverage, or if you do not thoroughly research your coverage options, you may be needlessly saddled with bills and expenses that will grow incrementally until your claim is settled a few years down the road.

How do you best arm yourself with full protection if you've had a collision? First, know your own insurance coverage. Second, discover the insurance coverage of every other party involved in the collision. This will take no small amount of time and effort on your part, but the long term financial paybacks are well worth the short term hassle of scrambling for copies of policies from all of the insurance companies involved.

Identifying Available Insurance Policies

Let's first take a look at some of the more common sources of insurance coverage and review the best ways for you to reap maximum benefits under these policies. Then we'll talk about a few of the less common sources of insurance coverage. These can be surprisingly lucrative cash sources that most people don't even think about in their frantic search for reimbursement after a traumatic automobile collision. It's much better to know about and tap all of your resources now, rather than face the disappointment later of getting too little, or nothing at all.

> **Your physical recovery should be your most important goal. Your financial recovery is important also, but what is financial health without the physical ability to enjoy it? Be aggressive about submitting claims for medical care. Your physical recovery today has a profound effect on the quality of your future life.**

Where to Begin Looking?

After the automobile collision, you need to look at all possible sources of insurance coverage. You should typically look first to the vehicles involved in the collision and then to the people themselves. This means that you should first investigate the insurance policies covering the at-fault driver's car, then pursue coverage under your own automobile policy. The next step is to review any insurance policies covering both drivers.

Let's start with automobile related insurance policies, then move on to policies that insure people.

PIP

Personal Injury Protection (PIP) coverage is a limited contract between you and your insurance company stating the benefits you will receive if you, family members or passengers in your car were injured in a collision, no matter who was at fault. PIP benefits may include payment for lost wages, medical bills, loss of services, home nursing care and even death and funeral benefits. Surprisingly, this outstanding coverage is one of the least expensive options on an insurance policy. It costs little to purchase. If you have a collision and make a claim against your PIP policy, your insurance company must begin paying your claims immediately.

After the collision, you may begin drawing on your PIP benefits to pay for hospital, medical, Chiropractic and certain out-of-pocket expenses. PIP pays a flat percentage of your normal wages or up to a maximum weekly amount, beginning on the fifteenth day following your collision.

Please see Chapter 3, "Personal Injury Protection" for additional information about this valuable insurance coverage resource.

Liability Coverage

The State of Washington requires all motorists to carry minimum liability insurance coverage of $25,000 per person. The fines and penalties for failing to have insurance while operating a motor vehicle are high. If involved in an automobile collision without insurance, you will automatically be fined. If you are at fault, you may lose your driver's license for up to three years or until you have made full financial reparations to any injured parties.

The law also requires insurance companies to offer uninsured motorist (UM) and underinsured motorist (UIM) coverage to every person purchasing liability coverage. An insured who chooses not to purchase UM or UIM coverage must decline the offer in writing.

Both UM (uninsured motorist) and UIM (underinsured motorist) coverage is provided to the policy holder by an insurance company. If your policy includes this coverage, you can submit a claim to your insurance company.

A driver is classified as "uninsured" when he or she injures another party in a collision and has no insurance to cover the damage caused. If you are damaged by such a negligent party, or "tortfeasor," your UM coverage will kick in and pay for damages that you suffered at the hands of the uninsured driver.

An "underinsured" driver is one who has liability insurance, but whose insurance policy limits do not cover the total damages incurred by the injured party. If you incur damages by the negligent acts of an underinsured motorist, you can receive payments for your damages from UIM coverage included in your insurance policy.

UM and UIM coverage can be a financial lifesaver if you are involved in a collision and your damages exceed the available maximum amounts payable under the other driver's insurance policy. For example, if the other driver's policy has a $25,000 payout limit and your damages and injuries total $65,000, the UM or UIM coverage on your policy may kick in and pay the additional costs up to the maximum amount provided by your insurance coverage.

Business Related Insurance

If either of the drivers was operating a vehicle while on the job, or if the car is owned by a business, then employer provided insurance should be investigated. Check into any insurance provided by union membership, employee associations or professional memberships. Also, if the collision occurred on business premises or because of the action of a representative of a business, business liability policies should also be examined for potential coverage.

Health Insurance

Your health insurance policy is a primary place to look if you are injured in an automobile collision and do not have medical benefits available on your automobile policy. Your health insurance carrier may pay for treatment of injuries and, depending on your policy, may pay for additional treatments, physical therapy, in home nursing, medical equipment and prescriptions. After you settle your claim with the at-fault driver, your health insurer may demand reimbursement from you or the third-party insurance company.

Homeowner's Insurance

Homeowner's insurance is another potential source of coverage. The policy language must be carefully reviewed to identify clauses that may provide payment for damage, loss or injury caused by a collision. Many people assume that home-owner's means that the collision or injury must have occurred within the insured home. This may not be true, and the homeowner's policy will reveal if your collision is covered.

Credit Disability

You will also want to look at any insurance coverage available through your credit cards. Many retailers and auto lenders provide disability or unemployment coverage on major purchases, and automatically bill a monthly premium for this coverage on your credit statement. These policies make minimum payments on the outstanding balance on your account if you are unable to work and pay your bills.

Mortgage Disability

Do you have disability coverage on your mortgage? Lending institutions customarily offer such coverage. If you are disabled or otherwise prevented from making your mortgage payments, the insurance policy steps in and continues to make mortgage payments to the bank while you cannot. It's important to submit a claim as soon as possible on a mortgage disability policy so that you can take full advantage of any time or payment limitations provided by your contract and avoid the financial and emotional trauma of possible mortgage default and foreclosure.

Other Insurance Options

We've discussed your insurance policies and the policies of the at-fault driver. You must not overlook another potential source of payment; the policies of spouses, family members, associates of yours and the tortfeasor. Also, you should investigate the insurance policies covering any person or entity whose action or inaction may be negligent. Perhaps the failure of a piece of equipment caused the collision, or there was a preventable hazard on the road due to faulty road design, missing road signs or inadequate lighting. These contributing factors could have been contributed by an individual, a business or a government entity. You will need to look at the "big picture" and identify who, if anyone, may have contributed to your collision.

Always review your own policy for language that supports your claim for payment.

If any other party or entity breached either a statutory or common law duty and that breach was a contributing factor to the collision, the insurance policies covering that party may be subject to your claim for damages.

Your Own Policy

How do you know if one of these insurance policies will reimburse you for damages? First, you need to look at the policy itself. Do not depend on the insurance agent representing the policy holder to advise you if the policy will cover the collision!

> **You should not rely solely on the representations of an insurance agent, adjuster, supervisor or underwriter. The final determination is found in the insurance policy itself. Only by reading the actual insurance policy can you successfully claim that you should be covered and to what extent. You should also be aware that common law or judicial rulings law may supersede the wording in the policy in favor of the insured.**

Contrary to what it may say in the marketing brochure, your own insurance agent may not be entirely committed to your best interests. Your agent is obligated to keep the cost of doing business, and that includes payments to you, to a minimum.

If you ask the other party for a copy of their insurance policy, your request may be ignored or refused outright. If this happens, call their insurance carrier directly and inform them that you are taking action against their insured and want a certified copy of the insurance policy or policies covering their insured.

> If you don't receive a response to your request, you have some options. First, be a "squeaky wheel" and make repeated and regular requests, both on the phone and in writing. Second, contact the Washington State Insurance Commission and file a formal complaint. Third, hire an experienced personal injury attorney and ask him or her to step in. That often produces an immediate response.

Policy Review Checklist

Once you get the policies, read all of the language contained in each policy and determine the following:

☐ Is the policy current? Was the policy in force on the date of the collision? Is the policy enforceable in Washington?

☐ Does the policy cover the tortfeasor and/or me?

☐ Are the circumstances of my collision covered by the policy?

☐ If I am at fault, does the policy still cover me?

☐ What will the policy pay for? (For example, lost wages, hospitalization, long-term disability.)

☐ What are the payout limits of the policy? Are there any time limitations, and should claims be submitted immediately?

Once you've identified additional tortfeasors and determined that their insurance covers your collision, you will need to prove that their negligence contributed to the collision and to your injuries. This will likely mean taking the tortfeasor and their insurance company to court. Immediately hire the best personal injury attorney you can find.

Be forewarned! Some insurance policies contain thousands of pages in bound book form. The process of translating voluminous insurance policies is unpleasant at best and sometimes impossible. Consider consulting with an attorney if you find yourself faced with the awesome task of deciphering reams of insurance industry legalese.

You may be able to successfully negotiate a settlement with an insurance company for payments from the at-fault driver's policy. However, if you are making claims against multiple tortfeasors for negligent acts that contributed to your damages, the intricacies and demands of negotiation and litigation pose a challenge well beyond your abilities and resources.

Consult an attorney if any of the following apply:

◆ You are seriously injured or in pain for months;

◆ You are restricted from working;

◆ You are making claims against more than one party;

◆ You have been in more than one accident;

◆ Negotiations and movement with an insurance company are stalled;

You are entitled to recover for "intangible" damages including pain and suffering, loss of enjoyment of life, past and future disability, permanency of injury and any future damages to your physical and financial health.

Determining Coverage for Injuries

If you're injured in an automobile collision, you typically look to the liability coverage in the at-fault driver's policies and to the UM/UIM and PIP coverage in your own policy. These cover all of your expenses or damages to put you back in the position you would have been in had you not been injured.

Items covered include medical bills, wage loss, out-of-pocket expenses, vocational retraining, general damages to cover your pain and suffering and any other incidental expenses whether they exist now or are likely to arise in the future.

Stacking Insurance Policies

Most people assume that they must choose between one policy or another when submitting claims for damages. However, in the State of Washington, there are occasions where it is legal to stack insurance policies. This means that you can submit the same claim to more than one insurance policy and receive payment on the claim from each insurer.

Stacking can be compared to buying multiple life insurance policies. These policies provide payment in the event of the death of the insured. Upon death, each policy will pay the stated benefit. It's no different with other insurance policies.

Some insurance policies contain language that prohibits stacking. Read policies carefully before purchasing and know the rights and benefits to which you are entitled.

You pay an insurance company to provide benefits in case of certain events. If you choose to pay more than one insurance company to cover you for loss, damage or injury, you may be entitled to receive the policy benefits from each insurance company if something bad happens.

If you are covered by multiple policies, prioritize the policies based on the size and extent of available benefits. Identify the policy with the most comprehensive, maximum coverage and submit your claims to that carrier first. Then, continue through the remaining policies and submit your claims in an order of priority that exhausts all available benefits. This process of prioritizing all available policies, called stacking, will provide you with maximum benefits and the opportunity to fully exercise your rights as an insured. However, be aware there may be statutory and common law rules that supersede the above stated strategy.

Stacking insurance policies can create coverage and billing nightmares. If you decide to retain an attorney to represent you, their office should handle all of the billing procedures, questions and disputes for you.

Insurance laws vary from state to state. Insurance stacking can be a complicated endeavor and it may be wise to contact a personal injury attorney versed in insurance law to ask him or her to step in.

When the Insurance Company Is Slow to Pay

Unlike some other states, Washington has no laws on the books that penalize an insurance company for damages incurred because it was slow in paying. Many insurance companies have a policy of delaying payment as long as possible. They can hold onto their cash and earn interest on it as they delay paying you. More importantly, they can often wear you down to the point where you could decide to drop your claim altogether.

The consumer is left with the short end of the stick in these situations. Even if lack of payment by an insurance company causes you to default on your mortgage, lose your business or fail to receive necessary medical treatment, you may not be able to claim any additional damages because of the financial and emotional harm caused by the insurance company's actions. If you take an insurance company to court for these reasons, you may only be able to claim the actual amounts that should have been paid in the first place. Retaining a skilled personal injury attorney can help speed up payment of benefits.

Determining Liability

The process of determining liability is a complex web of fact and circumstance. We can't adequately cover all of the issues of determining liability within the limited scope of this book. In short, liability, or who was at fault for a collision, must first be determined before most insurance benefits can be paid. It is always necessary to conduct your own immediate thorough accident investigation. Do not rely on others, except an experienced personal injury attorney team. Photos, measurements, witness statements and oftentimes expert accident reconstruction engineers are necessary.

If the insurance policy is a "no-fault" policy, you are paid regardless of liability. A good example is the typical health insurance policy. If you get hurt, regardless of the reason, your medical costs are covered. Most policies (automobile, homeowners and the like) have "no-fault" provisions contained in them as well as separate "at-fault" provisions which will not pay benefits until liability has been determined.

Are liability issues stalling payment of your claims? Then it may be time to call an attorney who can help expedite payment of your claims by the insurance company without a prolonged, costly courtroom battle.

The determination of fault can take months or even years and can ultimately end up in court. If your collision is not a cut-and-dried case of someone clearly doing something that caused damage, loss or injury to you, you may well encounter liability issues and denial of damages.

Always assume that the insurance company will attempt to assign fault to someone other than its insured. Remember that insurance companies are in business to make money, not pay it out. Police collision reports, eyewitness testimony, photographs and other exhaustive documentation may be necessary to prove that someone else was at fault.

Unfortunately, the final proof of liability is often only made successfully in court. When dealing with an insurance company on issues of liability, be prepared to take your case to court. You should hire a skilled attorney early in the case to ensure that critical evidence is accumulated and preserved.

Negotiating with the Key Players

When submitting a claim for payment to an insurance company, your typical frontline contact will be the insurance agent, either yours or that of other parties to the collision. The agent takes your report and submits your claim to the claims department. Once your claim lands there, you will be dealing with a claims adjuster. This individual "adjusts" how much money you are entitled to, based on the circumstances of the collision and the policy coverage. The adjuster may need to confer with the underwriting department, the folks who actually write the policies and determine coverage parameters.

If the agent or the adjuster is not able to answer your questions or respond to your requests satisfactorily, you may contact the underwriting department directly. However, be advised that you will typically get the same information and hear the same determinations from all of these individuals. They are, after all, working for the same company that is determined to hold onto its cash reserves.

> Throughout each step of your claim, you must provide complete documentation to support your claim and negotiate with the insurance company in person. As the injured party making a claim, the burden rests on you to prove the amount you are entitled to.

If you feel that the insurance company is not acting in good faith, contact the Washington State Insurance Commission and make a formal complaint. Be aware that if there is an investigation, it can continue over a long period of time and may not provide a finding on your behalf. If you want a more immediate response from an insurance company, call an attorney. Also, be aware that the Insurance Commission may not have the power to provide you with an acceptable remedy.

Insurance Reimbursement

When you successfully settle your claim with the responsible party's insurer (the third-party insurer), they will issue a check for the settlement amount. Your own insurer will typically make a claim against that third-party insurer and against any settlement paid to you. Your insurer will seek reimbursement of any amounts they paid to you for collision related losses.

Let's say the collision caused you to incur $10,000 in medical bills. You used a combination of your automobile PIP coverage and health insurance to pay these bills. You then successfully sued the negligent driver for $25,000. Your own insurance policies likely contain language that obligates you to repay the $10,000 your insurance companies paid on your behalf while you were negotiating a settlement with the third-party insurer.

Are you obligated to pay your insurance company the full $10,000? Probably not. It depends on the amount of coverage the at-fault driver has, the language in your own policies, and whether you have retained an attorney to assist you. You may be able to negotiate the amount of money your insurance company expects to be repaid. If you pursued and successfully managed to obtain a settlement from the third-party insurer, you should be entitled to some benefit for obtaining reimbursement for your first-party insurer. In Washington, there is now law that enables the injured victim, with the help of skilled counsel, to reduce the amount of the first-party insurance reimbursement.

Insurance companies are not enthusiastic about negotiating with their policy holders to reduce the amount of money they expect to be reimbursed. However, an attorney who is skilled in the art of negotiating with insurance companies may obtain a reduction in the amounts deducted from your settlement that will go to reimburse your first-party carrier, arrange that your attorneys' fees are paid from the insurance company's share of the settlement, and significantly increase the amount of money that you receive.

Negotiating a reduction in the amount due to your insurer can be tricky. Read your policy carefully and know your obligations. Negotiating with facts in hand and dogged determination may increase the settlement monies that land in your own pocket. Only an experienced personal injury attorney knows the negotiating strategies involved. If your injuries are serious, do not attempt representing yourself.

My law firm, Graham Lundberg & Peschel recently won a significant victory from the Washington State Supreme Court, and established new law in injury cases regarding how much insurance companies are required to reduce their reimbursement (subrogation) at settlement or judgment.

That case took us more than 10 years, fighting the insurance company (State Farm). As a result we are now involved in a class action against all insurance companies in Washington to recover past due subrogation amounts.

This is complicated and technical insurance contract work. If you have any delays or problems interpreting and enforcing insurance policies, call my firm or the best specialized lawyer in your neighborhood for assistance.

Bill Submission and Payment

Under most automobile policies, payment for medical bills is based on the following factors:

- The treatment must be for injuries sustained as a result of the collision. Prior conditions are not allowed, although exacerbation or aggravation of prior medical conditions may be.

- The treatment must be necessary; that is, it is required to return you to the same condition you were in before the collision.

Survival Guide *Checklist*

✓	Understanding Insurance Coverages
	Know your insurance policies!
	Be innovative when seeking additional coverage.
	Prioritize and stack insurance policies.
	Document! Document!! Document!!!.
	Investigate and obtain proof of liability early.
	Ask for HELP!!
	Identify the key players and give them what they need.
	Be politely persistent, disciplined and determined.
	If seriously injured, immediately hire the best personal injury attorney you can.

PERSONAL INJURY PROTECTION (PIP)

*I*n Chapter 2 we reviewed some of the common insurance policies that you should investigate for potential reimbursement of your claims. Throughout your quest for insurance coverage, no stone should remain unturned. In this chapter, we'll go into greater detail about one of the most effective sources of immediate financial reimbursement in the event you're injured in an automobile collision. Personal Injury Protection is a type of insurance coverage that every car owner should purchase.

The three fundamental rules involving PIP are:

♦ If injured, immediately apply for PIP benefits.

♦ Make sure all medical bills with accompanying records are submitted in a timely fashion and paid in full by PIP.

♦ Never attend a PIP requested medical exam without hiring the best personal injury attorney.

What is PIP?

Personal Injury Protection (PIP) coverage is a limited contract between you and your insurance company that describes certain benefits you will receive if you are injured in a collision, no matter who was at fault. PIP benefits may include payment for lost wages, medical bills, loss of services, home nursing care and even death and funeral benefits. These bills can be paid by the insurance company as they are accrued. Surprisingly, this outstanding coverage is one of the least expensive options on an insurance policy. It costs you little to purchase, and if you have a collision and make a claim against your PIP policy, your insurance company must begin paying you right away.

Why PIP?

PIP coverage promotes maximum physical recovery. It can protect you from the debilitating emotional trauma that can occur if you find yourself without adequate financial resources to protect you and your family from a sudden loss of income. Your physical recovery should be your top priority after an automobile collision. The faster you can get back on track financially, the better the chances that all of your energies, mental, emotional and physical, can more quickly be directed to healing and recuperation.

PIP coverage pays money to you regardless of who is at fault. People often mistakenly assume that the at-fault driver's liability coverage provides all one needs to pay for medical and other costs incurred because of an automobile collision injury. However, liability coverage may be withheld by the insurance company if you are found to be at fault in the collision.

PIP coverage is provided immediately following the collision. The at-fault party's insurance company will usually not pay for anything except property damage under liability coverage until it receives all of the reports and records about your collision and injury and reviews them for a final determination of any reimbursements. This could take months (or even years in some disputed cases).

One of the most important features of standard PIP coverage is payment for lost wages. This is the insurance industry's version of "disability insurance." If you're injured so badly that you are unable to work, a $200 per week cash benefit can very well be the difference between financial survival or disaster.

If you are injured on the job the State of Washington Department of Labor and Industries may provide a percentage of your lost wages as soon as 14 days after you submit an Initial Injury Report. The report must state that you are unable to work because of the injury. Because some claims take months to be accepted, you may qualify for provisional payments while your claim is being evaluated. Your PIP benefits may be affected if you are also claiming L&I benefits.

What if you are injured in a collision, are unable to work and can't pay your health insurance premiums? This is one of the most important reasons why you should have PIP coverage. PIP will pay you lost wages and provide the income that you need to continue to pay your health insurance premiums. Your health insurance covers your necessary medical care while you are settling your claim with the third party insurer. Under no circumstances should you allow your health insurance to lapse.

How Much Does PIP Pay?

PIP policies pay at least $10,000 in medical bills per collision and $10,000 for loss of wages or income if you are disabled from working. Washington State law now requires that all insurance companies offer a minimum of $10,000 of PIP coverage when they sell an automobile insurance policy. So important is PIP coverage that if you decline to purchase it, you must do so in writing.

> PIP coverage is included in your own automobile insurance. You can claim PIP benefits for you and your family when you're injured in an automobile collision while riding in your own or someone else's car. Any passengers who are injured in an automobile collision while riding in your car are also covered. PIP also covers you and your family as pedestrians.

An additional feature of PIP is that coverage is provided per collision. If you have more than one collision during the policy year, you may draw a total of $10,000 for the first collision, and an additional $10,000 for each collision during that year.

PIP policies can be purchased that provide up to $35,000 for medical for three years and $35,000 wage loss for one year. You should talk to your insurance agent about PIP coverage options that go beyond the minimum standards required by law.

After the collision, you may begin drawing on your PIP benefits to pay for hospital, medical, Chiropractic, therapy and certain out-of-pocket expenses. Most standard PIP policies pay 85% of your normal weekly wages, beginning on the fifteenth day following your collision up to a stated maximum. Your insurance carrier figures wage loss under your PIP coverage just like medical bills and out-of-pocket expenses. Payments stop when the maximum PIP coverage has been paid out.

Minimum PIP coverage is good for three years from the date of the collision. Do not delay making a claim under your PIP coverage, or you may lose the opportunity to take advantage of this excellent coverage.

Without PIP coverage, your medical and other related bills might remain unpaid until your case is settled. A year or more could go by before you see any money from the at-fault driver for lost wages, medical care and the like. In the meantime, you are faced with the frustrations of watching your savings dwindle, your credit suffer or perhaps mortgage foreclosure because you have no income due to a disabling injury.

Commercial automobile insurance policy may include "Med Pay" coverage. This type of coverage does not provide the protection of PIP. It is a medical payments only version of PIP, and doesn't cover wage loss or loss of services.

You may be unable to pay the medical bills that accumulate during your recovery. Past due bills can accrue finance charges that may not be reimbursed by the third-party insurer. It is not unusual to see thousands of dollars in medical bills following an automobile collision injury. Past due finance charges on these amounts can add up quickly. PIP coverage can provide the cash you need to make payments for your medical care before your case settles and avoid the additional expense of having to pay finance charges after settlement.

PIP and Your Insurance Company

Your insurance company (the first-party carrier) will track the payments made under your PIP coverage. If they question whether your medical treatment is reasonable and necessary, they may delay payment and request a records review or a medical exam. The PIP carrier must use an examiner who is licensed to practice in the same discipline or specialty as the healthcare provider who is treating you. Insurance companies call these Independent Medical Exams (IME). In no way are these independent; we call them defense medical exams. If the insurance company's doctor reports no objective findings of injury related to the collision, your PIP benefits may be terminated. Insurance companies want to keep their costs down and they will terminate your benefits if you can't quickly document your injuries to their satisfaction.

By law, your insurance premiums can't go up if you make a claim under your PIP coverage. Your PIP coverage exists to provide you with a ready source of funds to immediately pay your collision related expenses. Use it or lose it!

Be sure to follow your care provider's treatment plan to the letter, submit all bills, expenses and records to the insurance company immediately so that you quickly receive reimbursement under your PIP coverage for these expenses. Once you sign a settlement check offered by the third-party insurance carrier, your PIP benefits provided by your first-party insurance carrier stop. Make sure all of your financial losses are covered before accepting any settlement offer.

Your care providers should send the bills and records for your treatment directly to your PIP carrier. The insurance company requires itemized bills and chart notes. They will carefully review them to confirm that all of the treatments are related to the collision. The insurance company may also request that your care providers provide additional records.

If you or your care providers delay in providing a signed application for PIP benefits and authorizations for release of medical bills or records and/or employment to the insurance company, payments under your PIP coverage are likely to be delayed. If you are requesting reimbursement under PIP, you will need to carefully manage the distribution of appropriate information and communications between your insurance carrier and your medical team. This often requires follow up phone calls or letters by you to confirm that requested information has been sent and received in a timely manner.

If you have more than one collision in a given year and are making claims on your PIP coverage for multiple collisions, the injuries received in each collision and the respective costs incurred must be segregated. The insurance company treats each incident separately. You must carefully document and keep separate the treatment and resulting costs that are incurred for each respective collision. This can become extremely complicated, especially if you receive similar or related injuries in more than one collision.

To understand how PIP payments for multiple collisions may be applied, consider this scenario. You are injured on March 1st in an automobile collision. Under your standard PIP coverage benefits you will be paid for that collision for three years following the date of the collision, to a maximum of $10,000 each for medical expenses and lost wages.

Because this is going to be the worst year of your life, you are also injured in a second automobile collision on August 1st of that same year. PIP benefits are per collision. You can claim a maximum of $10,000 each for medical expenses and lost wages in benefits for the second collision for three years.

Let's say that the injuries that you received in the first collision on March 1st are successfully treated and you reach maximum medical improvement (MMI) seven months later on October 1st. When you reach MMI, your PIP medical coverage stops. The payments under your PIP coverage for this first collision totaled $3,500.

Even if you continue to receive treatment for the injuries received in the second collision on October 1st, you can't apply the "left over" benefits from the first collision to your treatment for the second collision. PIP benefits are paid per collision, and you can't combine treatment or benefits for multiple collisions.

Because of the complexities of multiple collision injuries, these cases often fail to settle and end up in court. If you have been injured in more than one automobile collision, consider the advantages of immediately retaining a personal injury attorney. He or she can assume the difficult task of managing your multiple claims and maximize your chances of achieving successful settlement without having to go to court.

If you are in a collision, your insurance agent may not volunteer that payments are available under your PIP coverage. However, Washington law mandates that your insurance company must inform you of the benefits available and the amounts. They can deny or limit your claim depending on their use of an IME. Be sure to ask your agent about your PIP coverage. If it's available, don't hesitate to submit claims for payment under that coverage.

The insurance industry relies on an unspoken truth: the great majority of Americans simply don't want to fight the system. Don't allow your fear of duking it out with the insurance companies to keep them in the Billion Dollar Club and leave you without needed benefits or fair compensation for damage, loss or injury. If you have PIP coverage, claim the benefits that are due you.

Your insurance company may not be aggressive about recommending that you accept the offer of PIP coverage now required by law. The money that your insurance company pays to you under your PIP coverage will be reimbursed later by the third-party insurance company (the insurance company that provided coverage for the at-fault driver). However, between the time your insurance company pays you money under your PIP coverage and when they are reimbursed by a third-party insurer, your insurance company is losing interest on that money. They, in effect, take a loss for the period of time before they are reimbursed.

If you don't have PIP coverage, or you're not certain if you do, call your insurance agent today and make sure this coverage is included in your policy. It's cheap protection!

> Payments under PIP coverage will only be made if the PIP coverage was purchased and in effect prior to the collision for which you are claiming coverage.

How Do I Claim My PIP Benefits ?

Here is the checklist that provides all of the steps that you must complete in order to take full advantage of your PIP coverage and receive the benefits that you need while receiving treatment for your injuries.

PIP Benefits Checklist

☐ Call your insurance agent to report the collision.

☐ Confirm that you have PIP or Med Pay.

☐ If yes, determine the time and dollar amount limits.

☐ Ask your agent to take your Report of Loss claim, phone in your report to the claims office and call you back with the claim number, address and phone number of the claims office.

☐ Call the claims office and get the name of the claims adjuster who is handling your claim. Ask the claims adjuster to mail the PIP Application, Attending Physician's Report and Salary Verification forms.

☐ Complete the PIP Application and sign the authorizations for release of medical records and employment records and return them to the claims adjuster.

☐ Have your doctor fill out the Attending Physician's Report and return it to you. Mail it to the claims adjuster.

☐ Have your employer complete the Salary Verification form and return it to you. Mail it to the claims adjuster.

☐ Provide your claim number and the adjuster's name, office address and phone number to all of your health care providers. Instruct your health care providers to bill your PIP carrier directly. Make sure they send chart notes with each billing statement.

☐ Continue to review and manage your health care to ensure efficient and timely receipt and payment on your claims for PIP benefits. Monitor all payments to make sure you aren't caught financially unprepared by the expiration of available PIP benefits.

☐ It is IMPORTANT that all of your treatment and diagnostic testing gets billed to PIP!

Plan Ahead!

When your PIP benefits expire (either after reaching maximum payout or maximum time limit under the policy), this is an opportune time for the third-party insurance carrier to increase the pressure on you to settle. They know that you may soon be experiencing a frightening financial crisis and will be more likely to settle soon and for far less than full value.

The best way to avoid getting yourself in such a losing situation is to plan ahead. Manage your treatment plan and recovery with an eye to the future. Ask your medical team to outline anticipated treatment and related costs early in your treatment plan. Involve your legal team. Make sure that both teams are communicating clearly and regularly. Compare the anticipated costs and duration of treatment with all of the combined insurance benefits that are available to you. If you have medical insurance, it may be available to pay for treatment covered under that contract or policy once your PIP benefits are exhausted. The medical insurer will require a letter from your PIP carrier advising that your benefits are exhausted as well as a completed incident report so they can set up a subrogation file to claim reimbursement out of any settlement proceeds. Be sure to have a personal injury lawyer review any reimbursement agreement from your health insurance company, before you sign and return it.

If early on in your treatment you determine that there is a chance that your PIP and other insurance benefits may run out before you'll be able to return to work and regain your financial security, you will need a law firm on your team. This projection needs to blended into the settlement negotiation strategy. Be prepared to hold out for as long as your medical treatment requires. Avoid the pitfalls of settling too early for too little because of mounting financial pressures.

If you realize that the insurance benefits that you've identified so far will not adequately cover your financial needs while you are negotiating a settlement, consider professional assistance. A personal injury attorney can often identify alternate sources of insurance benefits that you never even considered and help you manage the complexities of obtaining benefits from multiple insurance policies. In addition, settlement negotiations conducted by an experienced professional will often result in quicker settlement with a higher financial value.

When you have PIP coverage, your insurance company takes the financial loss while you are negotiating a settlement with the third party insurance company. If you don't have PIP, you take the loss. When your insurance agent offers PIP coverage, don't think twice—just do it!

Summary

The diligent consumer investing their insurance premium dollars year after year rarely gets a reasonable return on their investment in the insurance industry. Occasionally, however, changes occur in the industry that clearly benefit the consuming public. Personal Injury Protection coverage, now actively promoted by Washington State law, provides the consumer with a ready source of financial reimbursement during the time when it is often most desperately needed.

The substantial benefits available under even minimum PIP coverage often means financial survival for automobile, truck, cyclist and pedestrian collision victims. Know your insurance policies and use your PIP coverage to protect you and your family against the threats to your financial security that are so often generated by automobile collision injuries.

Survival Guide *Checklist*

✓	Personal Injury Protection (PIP)
	Always purchase PIP coverage.
	Start and use your PIP immediately after a collision.
	Don't hesitate to use your PIP coverage.
	Learn how to open your PIP claim..
	Make sure to get all of your treatment and diagnostic testing before PIP expires.
	Submit every medical bill to PIP for full payment.
	Plan your settlement negotiation strategy so that you're not forced to settle out of financial desperation.
	Never attend a PIP requested medical exam without an attorney.
	If seriously injured, immediately hire a personal injury law firm.

THE PERILS OF HANDLING YOUR OWN CLAIM

ow we come to what this book is really all about: whether to handle your own insurance claim. If you've come this far, then we haven't lost you in the gruesome horrors of automobile repair or the relentless nightmares of reading and understanding insurance policies. Don't worry—it gets better! In this chapter, we're going to provide an opportunity for you to really take a good look at yourself, your injuries and your resources and make an informed decision about whether or not you're a good candidate for handling, negotiating and settling your own case.

We've consolidated many years of experienced counsel and advice in this chapter and throughout this book. We believe that only a few seriously injured people can successfully negotiate their own settlement claim. In an effort to prepare you for what lies ahead as you determine whether to handle your own settlement claim, we'd like to give you as much knowledge and expertise as can possibly be included in the limited confines of a consumer resource guidebook.

Should I Represent Myself?

Anyone who is considering negotiating a settlement of their own claim should carefully read this chapter and decide, before taking the big plunge into self representation, if that is the most effective route to take. If you decide it's not for you, don't panic and feel that you're somehow inadequate. You're not alone. There are plenty of personal injury professionals who can handle your case for you and relieve you of all the demands, responsibilities and just plain work that self representation demands.

The legal system today is renowned for its complexity, delays and often overwhelming frustrations and confusion. Many people would try to convince you that you'd be a fool to jump right into settlement negotiations on your own, without the benefit of legal representation.

Once you've mustered the courage to represent yourself, you'll then have to commit a great deal of your time and energy to drive your claim through the many roadblocks, setbacks and stalemates that are the standard operating procedure of the insurance trade. You will only be successful if you are able to maintain a psychological, physical and spiritual balance throughout the settlement negotiations.

Some, but not many people, however, do just that. They manage to stay on top without sinking under the weighty demands of going up against the powerful insurance industry. The ones who do make it on their own do so for three very distinct reasons: they have the time, the temperament and the talent. You must have all three of these qualities, and in large doses, before you consider representing yourself.

The Three Major Qualifiers

There are few good reasons why you should represent yourself and settle your own insurance claim if you are seriously injured. Industry experts claim that a majority of all insurance settlements are made with people that are only slightly injured, who represent themselves. We call these folks "pro se."

Some slightly injured pro se claimants win close to full value settlements. People more seriously injured rarely accomplish a full financial recovery when they are pro se. It always boils down to the same three failures: they didn't have the time, the temperament or the talent to successfully represent themselves against the insurance machine.

Let's take a look at these characteristics. As you read the next sections, you are going to have to be very, very honest with yourself. Before you decide to represent yourself against an insurance company, you need to be absolutely certain that you possess all three personal characteristics. If you don't have these qualities and you do decide to take on the insurance industry, you will most likely be soundly stomped. When all is said and done, if you tackle self representation without adequate preparation and the required skills, you may find yourself in even worse physical and psychological condition after settlement than you were in before.

Do you need an attorney? To successfully negotiate your claim, or take your case to court and win, you need to answer with a resounding and confident "YES!" the following questions: "Do I have the time? "Do I have the temperament? and "Do I have the talent? If you answer no to any of these key questions, you would be better served by a competent legal counsel who has spent years developing settlement and litigation expertise.

Now is the time to examine your options, and make sure that you're in the best possible position when you take your serious injury claim to the insurance company.

Time

One of the primary reasons that insurance companies make so much money and pay out so little is that they learned long ago that if they hassle, badger, torment and just plain pick on the typical claimant hard enough, often enough and long enough, the claimant will finally break down and give up the good fight. Claimants soon reach that inevitable point where they throw up their hands and say, "That's it, I give up, I can't take this any more, just cut me the check!" Tis the sweetest song ever heard by the insurance adjuster!

Insurance adjusters are professionally trained in tactics and strategies that are specifically designed to stretch out your claim and your financial resources, weaken your emotional reserves and poke great gaping holes in your case. They blow you away and then they sweep you right into the corner of total surrender where, not too surprisingly, the adjuster is waiting for you with a settlement check in hand and a warm, understanding smile.

So how do you beat the insurance company at its own game? By putting time on your side. When you decide to represent yourself, you are making a large commitment of your free time or freeing up time otherwise committed to many different tasks that are required if you are to successfully settle your case.

Be A Telephone Junkie

From the time of your collision to the time of settlement you will need to make dozens, if not hundreds, of telephone calls. Start with calls to your insurance agent and probably the other party's insurance adjuster. Then calls must be made to the towing company, the storage yard and the car rental agency. You'll also be calling the auto body shop and other collision repair specialty shops. Phone calls to health care providers requesting appointments, follow-up care, records and billing information will also consume a large part of your settlement efforts. If your ability to remain employed is affected by the collision, you may also find yourself dealing on the telephone with your employer and other agencies that are involved in tracking and paying disability benefits.

Medical Care Team

If you are injured in the collision, there may be multiple care providers, such as a general practitioner, Chiropractor, neurologist, dentist, physical therapist or psychologist, to whom you will need to make telephone calls to arrange appointments, request tests and obtain test results. Transferring test results, X-rays and other medical documentation between the specialists handling your case must be carefully choreographed with upcoming appointments. Any time you make such a request, you should follow up with a confirming phone call to make sure your request was successfully handled. At each step in your medical care, you must notify the insurance companies handling the claim so that they can adjust their reserves accordingly and advise you of any coverage limitations.

Eyewitness Accounts

If there are witnesses to the collision, you will need to contact
these individuals immediately and arrange for supporting
documentation, written testimony or reports. Such witnesses
are often difficult to track after the collision, so it's important
that you contact them just as soon after the collision as
possible, either by telephone, letter or personal visit.

Documentation

One of the most important tools in your arsenal against
the insurance company is documentation. Photocopies,
photographs, written and signed statements, diagrams,
official documents and records, test results and anything and
everything that corroborates or supports your claim must
be gathered and presented to the insurance company as you
negotiate your claim.

Communicating with Your Employer

If the collision affects your ability to work, you must contact
your employer regularly to advise them of your status and
obtain the necessary sick leave, vacation time or unpaid leave
during your recovery.

Transportation

Keeping medical appointments, meeting with the appraisers,
making photocopies, meeting with eyewitnesses, retrieving
and dropping off medical supplies, rotating your car with a
rental car, dropping the kids off at child care while you attend
appointments... it can be an exhausting itinerary of driving
here, there, and everywhere to handle all the aspects of
your claim. If your medical care is neither well managed nor
scheduled early with the appropriate specialists, be prepared to
spend entire days traveling from appointment to appointment.

Daily Diary

Track and document each telephone call, appointment, interview or conversation in a record book. Do not make the mistake of depending on your memory. This is especially important if you have been seriously injured in the collision. Ten months down the line, the insurance company may demand ample and accurate documentation detailing all of the damages that you suffered because of the collision. Without accurate records, they may dispute your offhand recollection of what did or didn't happen during your recovery.

Do I Have the Time?

We're talking about time here, and lots of it, probably several hours each day. If you are working full-time, managing an active household or actively participating in retirement activities, you may not be able to meet the additional demands on your time that are generated by self representation.

If you were injured in the collision, you must remember that your physical recovery is of paramount importance. You must not rob from the time that has been set aside by your medical caregivers for rest, healing and recovery. To do so may delay your recovery, inevitably increase your medical costs and exhaust you physically, mentally and emotionally.

If you were pressed for time before the collision, think twice about committing time that you already don't have to pursue the complex and demanding claim process and eventual settlement negotiations This process will demand many hours each week.

Most importantly, if you were injured in the collision, think twice more about the potential damage you will be doing to your body and your mind if you undertake the stressful and demanding activities of self representation. The damaging effects may be permanent and no amount of settlement money will buy back your health and well-being.

If you can honestly say that you do have the time to conduct all of the activities that are required to settle your own claim, congratulations! You have passed the first test. Many people have courageously gone before you and have successfully managed the many demands of dealing with insurance companies one-on-one. If you are able to find the time, you may find that devoting that time to the settlement cause may result in successful settlement of your claim.

Temperament

What kind of person or personality wins a decent settlement from an insurance company? A persistent person! Someone who doesn't give up easily and who is not easily intimidated by professionally trained tacticians. When we're talking "temperament," we mean those qualities in a person that make him or her a suitable candidate for enduring long periods of frustration, denial and manipulation. The same qualities will compel the individual to take a personal stand and not waiver from it for one moment.

"Stubbornness" may seem a likely component of the "right stuff" for handling your own case. Surprisingly, it's flexibility that will prove to be your ticket to surviving the insurance scrimmage. You simply cannot let the tactics and strategies of the insurance company get to you. And remember that "getting to you" is exactly what the insurance adjuster is committed to doing.

You must be absolutely dogged in your determination to win. This does not mean that you should be abrasive, rude, hostile or dishonest. It does mean that you should be prepared to repeat your demands over and over and over again, and then just one more time for good measure, calmly, clearly and precisely. When they say "no," you must have the enthusiastic desire to turn that into a "maybe" and the willful determination to make it a "yes."

A person with the right temperament simply does not just "go away." You believe in your case, and nothing the insurance company says, does or threatens to do will dissuade you from your mission of a fair settlement. You must marshal all of the required documentation, testimony and test results and use them creatively to support your case.

The facts are presented in a factual manner and so too, are the emotional aspects of your claim. The people with the "right" temperament are not apologists. They are able to articulate and substantiate their complaints without feeling uncomfortable that others may think they are "whining." In a reasonable, logical and adult manner, those individuals communicate their demands clearly and believe in the value of their claim.

Changing Temperaments

Temperament, of course, can change over time. We may begin the claims process and eventually settlement negotiations coolly and calmly, and after a month or two of beating our heads against the Walls of Insurance, there may be a ragged edge to our voice and a peculiar gleam in our eye. Certainly, nobody is completely immune from the effects of taking repeated abuses from any quarter, least of all from an insurance company. But the person with a suitable temperament for self representation must be able to endure rigors and slide through the many hassles (both perceived and real) that go with the territory, keeping the aim on the goal of successful settlement.

One's natural temperament can also go through drastic changes after severe injuries. A slowly healing injury and unremitting chronic pain can prevent even the most Herculean survivor from functioning at their former level headed, good-natured and rational self. Financial stresses, bill collectors, family tensions, inability to exercise, weight gain or the inability to perform on the job or even stay employed at all, can all have disastrous effects on one's physical, mental and spiritual well-being.

If you have been injured in a collision, even your fabulously sterling personality can undergo changes that may adversely affect your ability to handle the stresses and demands of self representation. Again, your physical recovery is the most important thing following an injury collision. You will need to put all of your personal resources into recovery after the collision. Committing even a fraction of those resources elsewhere may not be the smartest thing to do.

Do I Have the Temperament?

While you may have been a perfect candidate for self representation before the collision, think carefully about your state of physical and mental health now before committing so much of yourself to what may be an extended period of claims processing, building your case through documentation and settlement negotiations. Are you feeling stressed? Depressed? Angry? Are you experiencing pain, or are your abilities limited because of the collision? Are you dealing with family tensions, employment stresses or financial difficulties? Any one of these situations can dramatically impact your ability to maintain the right frame of mind while you are pursuing your claim.

Remember that the typical insurance company has unlimited time, unlimited resources and an unlimited desire to win. If your injuries make it doubtful that you can compete on their level, do yourself a favor: don't even try, hire the best personal injury attorney you can find.

If you're convinced that you've got the time and the temperament, you've almost got the winning combination to handle your own case! Let's take a look at the last and probably most important attribute: Talent. Everybody has some, but let's see if yours is the right kind.

Talent

When talking about "talent," let's focus on the skills and abilities that dictate the difference between success and failure in building, managing and strategizing an insurance claim, eventually entering settlement negotiations. Just about everyone thinks of themselves as a decent negotiator. You get a good deal here, a great buy there. The truth is, however, that truly good negotiation skills don't come naturally. They're learned, developed and honed to precision only after years of experience marked by some failures and many successes. Successful resolution starts at the day after the accident. It requires organization, communication, discipline, determination, follow through and more organization.

This is where the average lay person and the insurance company are most at odds. The insurance company is dedicated to two things: obtaining control and maintaining control. They are able to do this because they are excellent negotiators and skilled tacticians. They know the claims business inside and out. It's not often that the average person has the same scope and depth of negotiating experience.

If you are unable to grab control of your claim straight out of the gate, it is highly unlikely you will ever be able to wrestle it from the insurance company somewhere down the line.

Once lost, it's almost impossible to regain control during the settlement negotiations.

Typically, an insurance company will assign an adjuster to close your claim in 48 hours. If that is not accomplished, your case may be assigned to another adjuster, who specializes in closing claims in five days or less. If on the fifth day your case isn't closed, yet *another* adjuster steps in. He is assigned the responsibility of closing your case in two weeks. After him comes the next adjuster, who is the one month specialist. And so on. Each of these individuals will use professional, practiced sales techniques on the unsuspecting consumer. They know all the angles. They know exactly what to say to convince and sometimes badger the claimant to sign on the dotted line and close the claim.

Do I Have the Talent?

Within the limited scope of this book we cannot teach you the negotiating skills that you need to survive and win against the insurance giants. However, if you have professional training or experience in negotiating, including setting strategies and planning specific tactics, you may well possess the third and most crucial skill, the talent for negotiating, that will ensure successful self representation.

If you do not have this kind of experience under your belt and cannot use it when the going gets hot and heavy, you may lose some extremely important bargaining points in the process. Once this happens, you're likely to end up watching helplessly as the settlement amount of your claim suffers.

We've covered the three major attributes of the winning settlement claimant: **time, temperament** and **talent**. If this successful combination describes you, then congratulations! You're a natural winner! You'll most likely prevail against the insurance company. Put everything you've got into your case, stay focused, remain truthful, don't be dissuaded by threats and stalling techniques and document, document, document! Take it to the wall and win!

How Does the System Treat Pro Se Claimants?

So you've decided to represent yourself. Welcome to the community of competent people like you who have the abilities to state their case and stick to their guns. There are some things you should know and apply as you begin your journey down the road of self representation.

Medical Providers

You must be diligent throughout your medical care! Medical specialists do not often communicate with specialists in other fields. For example, unless you proactively manage your medical care, your Chiropractor may not know what your neurologist has already diagnosed. This may lead to lapses in treatment that will prove to be damaging to your health and may increase your medical costs as well. You must assume the responsibility of making sure that all the important information is shared among your medical providers. If one specialist asks for test results from another, it's up to you to make sure the results get delivered.

If you experience symptoms or problems following a collision, you must be consistent about communicating this to your medical providers. While your dentist may not be interested in the numbness in your hands, your neurologist will. Be aware of the various specialties. Volunteer all relevant information to the appropriate medical provider, and seek additional medical care from an alternative source if the situation demands it.

Insurance Carriers

As discussed in Chapter 2, you must be especially attentive to the various policies and coverage provided by all of the insurance carriers that are parties to your claim. Insurance companies are less likely to take seriously those injured persons who represent themselves. Insurance professionals know that exerting the negotiating strategies of getting and maintaining control will more likely be effective against the average guy on the street than against an attorney.

Insurance companies have large financial reserves with which they can retain professional legal counsel. As a pro se claimant, you will be up against some very experienced litigators. The insurance companies hire attorneys who specialize in fighting legal issues in court. They are adept at persuading the jury and presenting the facts in the light that is least favorable to you. The jury may like you and they may even believe you, but in the hands of a skilled courtroom tactician, your side of the case may be quickly clouded if not entirely forgotten by the time the defense attorney is finished presenting the insurance company's side of your case.

> Just because you have chosen to appear pro se does not mean you receive special considerations. It only means that you receive the same considerations as the legal professionals who have studied and practiced the law for many years. You must be prepared to know and meet all of the legal requirements if you choose to represent yourself. Ignorance is no excuse. This applies both during the settlement negotiation phase and during any courtroom litigation, should your case reach that point.

Judges and Court Personnel

The legal code of ethics demands that attorneys and others in the legal profession give the same, or greater, consideration and respect to individuals who are representing themselves. However, the legal code, Latin and all, also applies to *you* when you represent yourself.

While there are some instances in American folklore where the "underdog" is looked upon kindly by the judge and jury, in today's legal system this simply doesn't happen. The courts are stretched beyond capacity and there are extraordinarily specific rules, regulations and deadlines that *must* be followed to the letter. For example, if you miss a deadline to submit a brief (a type of legal document) to the court, the judge may not read it at all and it may mean you lose your case.

Your preparation (including comprehensive documentation), well-groomed professional appearance and attention to every detail will send the message that you are to be taken seriously. An articulate, persuasive, consistent and honest approach to all aspects of your case will lend additional credibility to your claim. Together, all of these things create the winning combination that produces a successful settlement.

But what should you do if you have honestly assessed your abilities and limitations and have discovered that you may not have what it takes to successfully settle your own claim?

When Do I Need an Attorney?

Just as there are many reasons to settle your own insurance claim, there are also some compelling reasons why you should *not*. We've talked about time, temperament and talent, and how important they are to your successful claim.

It needs to be said: there are certain cases that simply must be handled by a competent personal injury professional. If you have been representing yourself up to this point and you suspect that now you may need an attorney, it may *not* be too late to hire an attorney to assume your case and pursue the highest value for your claim.

The first step is to select an attorney and call him or her and briefly outline your case on the telephone. Ask for an initial consultation. Confirm that the initial consultation is free. If it is not, consider another attorney.

The experienced personal injury attorney will meet with you and discuss the details of your case. Often, the attorney will advise you that there is no need for you to obtain legal counsel. The attorney should be able to provide some basic guidance during the consultation that will help you continue to successfully manage your own claim.

Sometimes, the attorney will evaluate your case and determine that it is too late for legal representation to have a significant impact on your case. Perhaps you already released information to the insurance company already that has irreparably compromised your case. Maybe you neglected to use certain insurance benefits before they expired.

Additionally, you may have already arrived at a settlement amount that cannot be raised significantly by the intervention of an attorney. In this situation, a competent attorney will advise you to take the offered settlement now, without legal representation. An attorney coming into the picture so late in the game may not increase the settlement value and may actually decrease it because of attorney's fees.

However, certain situations following an automobile collision may require that you hire an attorney. Following are some warning signs that may indicate it's time for you to call a personal injury attorney now.

If You Were Injured in the Collision

Even a seemingly minor injury or discomfort can turn into a major medical expense later on and may seriously affect your ability to work. If you have any suspicion that you were injured in the collision, you need the support of a legal professional who is experienced in assessing the claim value of your injury and managing your medical care, billing and continued insurance coverage.

If You Have No Insurance

Many people mistakenly think that if they have no insurance, an attorney won't handle their case. Wrong! If you don't have first-party coverage (your own insurance policy), you won't have the advantage of having an insurance professional represent your insured losses. You need someone in your corner to protect you from the devastating physical and financial losses that can occur. If you don't have insurance of your own, it's easy to think that you're up the proverbial creek when it comes to getting monetary reimbursement from an insurance policy. But an attorney can step in immediately to represent you and deal directly with the at-fault driver's insurance company to protect your interests.

If the Other Driver Has No Insurance

It is difficult tracking down the financial assets and recoverable funds of an uninsured driver. An attorney is more experienced than you in ferreting out the potential resources and possible alternative insurance policies (see Chapter 2) that may provide compensation for your injuries and losses.

When the Insurance Company Asks for a Recorded Statement About the Collision

Insurance companies are prepared to ask you leading questions that may elicit responses that may not be to your advantage when it comes time to settle. Especially in situations where fault is questionable, your statements may persuade an insurance company to place blame for the collision on you and thus diminish the value of your claim.

Anticipate that the insurance company will ask for a statement and prepare a written statement ahead of time. Your "script" should contain the basic facts of the collision, a concise narrative of your injuries and a chronological history of the medical care that you received as a result of the collision.

You would be amazed at how a simple response, such as "Oh, I'm doing OK" can sound in court. These words out of context sound like you were perfectly all right after the collision and suffered no injuries whatsoever. Your statements may be interpreted later as enthusiastic affirmations that you suffered no damages as a result of the collision, thus significantly reducing the value of your claim.

When the Insurance Company Asks You to Sign an Authorization to Release Medical Records

The insurance company will try to convince you that you must sign an authorization. Your own insurance company may tell you that if you don't sign the authorization, you are breaking the terms of the contract and they will drop your coverage. The truth is, you do not have to sign a blanket authorization for all medical records. Never do this! This allows an insurance company unlimited access to your old medical records, some of which may negatively affect your case. (How about that psychotherapy in 1994? Or the inpatient treatment for alcoholism in 1996?)

Rather, you should authorize release of only those medical records that apply *directly* to the collision. That is, between the date of the collision and the date the authorization is signed.

It is not always easy signing a limited authorization for the insurance company. This is one situation where you may need the assistance of an attorney.

If You are Having Difficulties with Your Own Insurance Company

If your own insurance company is stalling or otherwise giving you problems, this is *not* a sign of good things to come! Remember: you paid those insurance premiums for contracted coverage in the event you had a collision. While an insurance company may be slow to respond to an individual claimant, they are surprisingly responsive when an attorney picks up the phone and gives them a friendly jingle.

If Your Insurance Company Requests an Independent Medical Examination (IME)

If your insurance company requests that you see one of their contracted medical examiners, do not under any circumstances agree to go without first obtaining legal consultation. The doctor hired by your own insurance company may likely testify against you, because the doctor is hired by the insurance company to reduce the amount of money that the insurance company may have to pay on your claim. Remember, insurance companies are in the business to make a profit.

If the Other Driver's Insurance Company is Out of State

This is a red flag that often means you will be dealing with a substandard insurance company that may be operating under laws different from those in the State of Washington. Typically, you will be faced with extensive written correspondence and lengthy long distance calls when attempting to communicate with these companies. The old adage, "Out of sight, out of mind," applies all too frequently in these situations. If you are unable to deal in person with your adversary, your negotiations will suffer.

If the Collision Caused a Minimal Amount of Property Damage

The lower the property claim, the bigger the problem. Sounds odd, doesn't it? There's a simple reason for this warning: the insurance industry is extremely vigilant when it comes to fraud. When someone files a claim for injuries, and the damage to the automobiles involved is either minimal or nonexistent, the insurance company begins to wonder how your claimed injuries could have happened when property damage was so minimal. A big red flag goes up in the adjuster's office and comes right back down onto the cover of your file: FRAUD!

Insurance companies have special investigative units that are highly funded and specifically focused on identifying and prosecuting insurance fraud.

Sometimes an innocent plaintiff gets involved in fraud investigations because they unknowingly go to a medical practitioner who has already been targeted because of possible fraudulent medical practices. If your case ends up being investigated for fraud, you will have a battle on your hands trying to convince the insurance company that your case is legitimate. You must have an attorney direct your claim away from the fraud division and back into the claims mainstream where it will be evaluated fairly and settled reasonably.

If You Had a Pre-existing Medical Condition

Insurance companies love to jump on the "pre-existing bandwagon." They will insist that any injuries you are claiming now are, in fact, old injuries that you've had forever. If they get their hands on old medical records that document a pre-existing condition, you may have a tough time compelling the insurance company to ante up any money for medical treatment or other damages.

An experienced attorney will know how to present your injuries in the collision separate and apart from any other pre-existing conditions. Also, an accomplished legal professional can implement the "egg shell" theory. This in essence says that if you hit someone who already has a very fragile skull and crack their head, you have committed no less a serious injury to that person than if you'd hit someone with a head like Hulk Hogan. The person with the fragile head is hurt even worse than the healthy person, and the at-fault party is responsible for the more serious injuries.

Contrary to what the insurance industry would like us all to believe, people with pre-existing conditions do not cruise the highways and slam their brakes in search of convenient ways to exacerbate their injuries and relive the pain and disability they suffered in an earlier collision!

If You're Just Not the Same Old You

Last, we include the final indicator of when you should hire an attorney. We call this the "On the Edge" test. Have you lost your sense of humor? Are you depressed because you can't work or play like you used to before the collision? Does every little thing take you to your wit's end? Do you feel like everything is piling up and you can't see your way out from under the mounting stress? Do you feel like you're living in some strange and scary place where NOTHING is going right? Then you need an attorney to help alleviate the stress of a collision injury before it destroys the quality of your life now and in the future.

How Can an Attorney Help Me?

If you decide to hire an attorney, you will want to read Chapter 5. That chapter goes into much greater detail about finding an attorney and working with him or her throughout your personal injury case.

For purposes of this chapter, let's review some of the basic ways that an attorney can help you to determine the highest claim value for your case, obtain the best settlement and return you to your physical, mental and emotional state of health prior to the collision.

Controlling the Case

A qualified personal injury attorney can literally take control of your case and dictate the timing, manner, tone and substance of the case. This is exactly what the insurance company will do to you if not adequately represented. With competent representation, the tables are turned. Negotiations cease to be one-sided in the insurance company's favor.

Managing the Care Providers

Your attorney acts as the "executive" who oversees all aspects of your medical care. Because medical specialists don't often communicate across the lines of their own specialties, an attorney can provide the communication and coordination between different practitioners. This can mean the difference between inadequate or inappropriate care and comprehensive, proactive and complete care. Also, many times a patient simply can't, or forgets to, communicate important things concerning what is going on with their bodies or their minds after a collision.

The patient may be physically or emotionally unable to manage all of the demands presented by multiple care providers. This is especially true if the patient is seriously injured or has suffered a head injury that limits their ability to think clearly or function at 100% capacity.

Managing Medical and Other Bills

The typical injury causing automobile collision generates voluminous forms, authorizations, records, statements and bills. These must be received, appropriately processed and filed in a timely manner. A skilled attorney and his or her support staff will gladly undertake the management of the "paperwork mountain" as part of your overall case. Most people cave in to insurance demands for early and inadequate settlement because they simply can't manage the day-to-day paperwork generated by a typical settlement claim.

If insurance billings are delayed or improperly paid, medical providers are not paid promptly and they inevitably put pressure on the patient. This is the last thing you need if you are already dealing with other stresses caused by the collision! Turning this over to your attorney means peace for your mind, and a stress free healing and recovery time for your body.

Persuading the Insurance Company

A legal professional skilled in personal injury cases is experienced in the art of negotiation and persuasion. With the added support of extensive law office personnel, an attorney can present a professional and effective case to the insurance company. Professionally written correspondence, effective graphical documentation, descriptive videotapes, compelling witness interviews, PowerPoint presentations and effective management of insurance company ordered medical examinations are the strengths of a winning settlement claim. These highly effective negotiating tools are "second nature" to an experienced personal injury lawyer.

Fearlessly Advocating for the Client

An attorney who specializes in personal injury has many years of experience working with injured plaintiffs, insurance companies, medical providers, employers and all the other parties that are drawn into the vortex of your automobile collision, injury and recovery.

It's "heads up!" time if you are facing physical pain and recovery, emotional trauma, family stresses or if your economic livelihood is threatened or ended altogether, or if you can no longer enjoy the pleasures that before the collision brought the good things your way. It may seem like everything that could possibly go wrong is coming down on you when you can least handle it on your own.

Your attorney can speak for you and act on your behalf, insulating you from the additional traumas and stresses caused by everyone wanting something from you that you simply are unable to give while you are recovering from your collision.

Once you have established a trusting, open and cooperative relationship with your attorney, he or she will prove to be your "best friend" throughout the ups and downs of your recovery and settlement process. A good personal injury attorney is comforting, reassuring and supportive, yet is able to deal aggressively and convincingly with the insurance companies.

Actually, multitasking is what a personal injury attorney does second best. What your attorney will do best of all is look out for your interests and maximum settlement value during all phases of your settlement negotiations.

Summary

In our personal injury practice, we talk and meet every day with people who have tried to settle their own insurance claim and for one reason or another have become convinced that they're stuck, they just can't do it any more and they want us to step in and take over. We review their claim with them and talk a little bit about how they've been conducting their negotiations with the insurance company. Of course, we do meet some folks who are truly stuck, either because theirs is a complex case or they simply are physically or emotionally unable to handle the demands of representing themselves.

But you'd be surprised how often we're able to quickly identify just what is needed to improve their strategy and produce a successful settlement. With a few words to the wise and some helpful, supportive guidance, we're able to put many people back on track and send them on their way to their own successful claim settlement, without professional legal representation.

If after reading this chapter you decide that you are a good candidate for negotiating your own settlement claim, then we've succeeded in doing what we set out to do when we wrote this book. You're likely feeling ready and enthusiastic about reading the rest of this guide, developing your most effective strategies and negotiating the highest possible value for your claim. Perhaps most surprising of all, you'll have fun doing it!

Survival Guide *Checklist*

✓	The Perils of Handling Your Own Claim
	Look before you leap—self representation isn't for everyone.
	Honestly assess whether you have the time, temperament and talent for self representation.
	If you decide to represent yourself, understand that you will be held to the same standards of preparation and professionalism as an attorney.
	Write out a statement covering how the collision occurred, your injuries, treatment and wage loss, and always stick to it.
	Quick settlements are rare; prepare to negotiate.
	All cases require extensive organization and document management.
	Know when to ask for help.
	Know the warning signs that earmark your case for negotiation difficulties.
	Consult with an attorney early to determine your case needs.

FINDING THE RIGHT ATTORNEY

reviously you learned how to determine if you should handle your own case. In this chapter, we will assume that you are not going to represent yourself and that you need to find a personal injury attorney. You'll learn how to evaluate that attorney and his team to see if they are qualified to handle your case.

We're going to encourage you to ask many important questions, including:

♦ Has your doctor's office worked with the law firm with good results?

♦ What is the size of the support staff? Is the team experienced in working on cases like yours?

♦ Does the legal team have a department dedicated to coordinating and disseminating medical information to your providers? Can they get all of your bills paid promptly?

We'll also cover some of the typical fees and costs of personal injury representation and identify the arrangements that provide the maximum financial benefit for you.

What is a Personal Injury Attorney?

There are many different specialties in the field of law. Some attorneys limit their practice to tax cases, others specialize in business law and there are a great number who specialize in family law, which includes divorce and child custody. Most attorneys, however, don't specialize in a particular area. Just like many doctors who provide comprehensive, general care to their patients, we call these attorneys general practitioners. They provide a much needed source of legal expertise and advice to their clients for wide ranging legal matters.

You may have worked with an attorney who provided great legal advice on that real estate deal in 2003. It may well be that the family law attorney who handled your divorce is a terrific lady and a real go-getter in the courtroom. But if you have been involved in an automobile collision, especially one in which you have been seriously injured, it's important to consult with an attorney who has many years of focused experience in the field of law that deals with automobile collision litigation. These attorneys are specialists in personal injury or PI for short.

If you have been injured in an automobile collision and even if you have already decided to settle your case on your own, schedule a consultation with an experienced personal injury attorney. During the initial interview, an experienced PI attorney will review your case and provide basic guidance free of charge.

Finding a Good Referral

There are a few tried-and-true ways to find a good personal injury attorney. There are also some pitfalls to avoid.

The most effective way to find a good, reputable personal injury attorney is to ask people you know and trust. Family, friends and business associates may have personal experiences working with a personal injury attorney. Your employer may be able to recommend a personal injury attorney with whom your company has had contact on behalf of an injured employee.

When you ask trusted family members or friends to recommend a personal injury attorney, get curious! Ask them about their personal experience with the attorney. A few of the questions you may want to ask are summarized below.

Attorney Referral Checklist

☐ Did the attorney keep promises to call back and take appropriate action?

☐ Was the attorney professional, efficient and readily available?

☐ Did the attorney regularly communicate with the client, providing informative phone calls, letters and reports?

☐ Did the settlement proceed smoothly and in a timely manner or did it seem to drag on without any resolution in sight?

☐ Did the case go to trial, and if so, did an experienced legal team handle the trial litigation?

☐ Did the attorney win a satisfactory settlement or a good outcome at trial?

☐ Were the attorney's fees and costs reasonable?

☐ Was the injured person satisfied with the experience and happy with the outcome?

☐ Would the injured person go back to that same attorney to handle another personal injury claim? If not, why not?

In addition to family and friends, another excellent source of good referrals is your medical practitioner. If you have been injured in an automobile collision and want to talk to an attorney about your case, ask your medical caregiver to recommend a law firm. Most likely, your doctor has had experience working with personal injury attorneys and can recommend a good one.

> Places to avoid when seeking a referral to a personal injury attorney are television and radio advertisements. Many of these commercials are produced out-of-state and offered "cooperatively" to attorneys throughout the country. Such advertisements may indicate that a particular attorney is experienced in personal injury. As you will quickly learn, more than limited experience is required to qualify an attorney to successfully settle your claim.

Remember that your medical caregivers and your attorney will work together with you as a team to negotiate a successful settlement. If your doctor has already experienced professional, courteous and competent contact with a personal injury attorney, she will be happy to share that referral with you and you will become part of an established, successful team.

Your First Phone Call

Your first point of contact with a prospective personal injury attorney is likely to be a telephone call to his or her office. This first contact is important. The following checklist will help you to decide at that point if it's worth your while to visit the attorney for an in person evaluation of your case.

- Was your telephone call answered promptly, without a busy signal, prolonged hold or diversion to voice mail?

- Was the receptionist courteous, professional and willing to direct your call promptly to the appropriate attorney or paralegal?

- Did the attorney or paralegal to whom you spoke give you their undivided attention on the phone?

- Did the attorney or paralegal clearly and without hesitation provide a satisfactory rundown of the attorney's qualifications for handling personal injury cases?

- Did the attorney or paralegal ask you specific questions about your case? For example:

  1. What was the date of the collision?

  2. Were you injured?

  3. What medical care have you obtained?

  4. Do you require additional medical care?

  5. What insurance is available?

- Did the attorney or paralegal offer to set an appointment for you to come in and discuss your case, free of charge, to obtain the necessary information to fully evaluate your case?

If you can answer "yes" to all of the above questions, then you are probably on the right track toward finding a qualified personal injury attorney team.

Warning Signs!

Warning signs that you are on the wrong track include:

- An office staff that is not enthusiastic or helpful or seems inconvenienced by your call.

- You find it frustrating or impossible to get to a "live person" or your phone calls go unreturned.

- Once you are put in touch with an attorney or paralegal, they do not give you their undivided attention (put you on hold, carry on side conversations, continue to munch that extraordinarily crisp green salad…).

- The attorney or paralegal waits for you to ask all the questions, without initiating a thorough, preliminary screening of the facts of your case.

- Straight off the bat, the attorney or paralegal suggests a high dollar value to your case and makes promises of getting a fast cash settlement for you. *This is a significant warning sign that you are not dealing with a professional operation!*

The Initial Consultation

If the attorney passes your first telephone contact with flying colors, you can now proceed to the next step: the free initial consultation, probably held in the attorney's office. This provides you with a second and more effective opportunity to assess firsthand the attorney's qualifications and ability to be your best representative.

When you arrive at the initial consultation, ask yourself the following questions:

Is the main office area clean, organized, and professional appearing? Personal injury cases require tremendous amounts of paperwork, forms, reports and the like. A disorganized office means disorganized files. When you have deadlines to meet and legal papers to file on time, you don't want your attorney wasting precious time trying to track down lost paperwork in a cluttered office.

If you are invited to an initial consultation and informed that you will be billed an hourly charge, decline the invitation and continue your search. Any injury attorney worth his salt will provide the first consultation free of charge and advise you during that consultation whether or not you need an attorney to handle your case. It's free advice, and it's good advice.

Were you greeted professionally by a designated staff person upon your arrival? The receptionist is the first point of contact for most businesses. Consequently, a professional business will put great effort into hiring personable, professional front office staff. If the receptionist is unprofessional, disinterested or discourteous, you know right away that this is an office that doesn't care about how it treats its clients and it won't care about how it treats your case.

Were you made to wait beyond your designated appointment time in a crowded waiting area? If you've been asked to wait a few minutes for your appointment, there is probably no reason to worry. However, if you've been sitting more than a few minutes and nobody bothers to give you an update on your appointment time, be wary. If there are others like you in the waiting area who are inconvenienced by a delay in their scheduled appointment time, this is a sign of a poorly run office that has little regard for the comfort and convenience of clients.

Does the office staff appear professional? Do they seem enthusiastic and positive about their jobs? These people are the folks who will be handling many of the day-to-day, administrative activities of your case. A law office that cares about the well-being and satisfaction of its employees automatically apply that same concern to its clients.

Assessing the Initial Interview

Once you have been introduced to the paralegal or attorney who is conducting the interview, you have the next and last opportunity to assess the attorney's qualifications to handle your case. Some preliminary questions that you should ask yourself are:

Were you adequately introduced to the attorney handling the interview? Did the attorney greet you by name? If not, then you may be speaking with someone who does not put a great deal of effort into even the most basic details. During settlement of a personal injury case, details matter.

If staff members appear unmotivated or just downright unhappy, move on to another attorney and a working environment that says "We are winners!" In both words and actions.

In Washington State, many law firms now employ paralegals to perform legal activities that were previously performed only by attorneys. Qualified paralegals have years of advanced training plus several years of professional law office experience. If you are interviewed by a paralegal rather than an attorney, evaluate the paralegal's professional demeanor just as you would an attorney's. After all, a paralegal works closely with the attorney and will likely reflect the attorney's own professionalism.

Is the office used for the interview comfortable, neatly organized and private? First impressions are lasting ones. If you're uncomfortable during the interview figure out why and take note that your discomfort may continue through the duration of your relationship with this particular attorney.

Is the attorney familiar with the facts of your case that you provided over the telephone? If you have to repeat everything, then you are encountering either a breakdown in communications or inattention to detail. Both are warning signs of things to come.

Did the attorney provide a quick background of his or her qualifications and the history of the law firm? Professional pride in accomplishments and expertise should be evident. The attorney should gladly share with you some background on his or her own practice and the practice of the law firm as a whole. Most lawyers will be able to provide you with a firm brochure, other publication or web site that explains their area of practice and provides some historical background. If the attorney does not offer this information, ask the important questions listed in the Qualification Checklist below and form your opinion based on their responses.

Does the attorney voluntarily explain to you what you can expect? The anticipated time frame for settling your case, the attorney's anticipated activities and responsibilities, and your responsibilities should be clearly spelled out. The attorney should have a good feel for the work that your case will entail, and should voluntarily provide that information to you.

That Old Familiar Feeling

It sounds silly, but it's true: trust your gut instinct. If during the initial meeting you like what you see and hear, do a quick internal check and ask yourself how you feel about the person on the other side of the desk.

You should be wary of the attorney who offers a quick dollar value of your case. A competent personal injury attorney will carefully evaluate all aspects of your case, wait until you have reached maximum medical improvement and then provide a settlement range that will form the guidelines for negotiation with the insurance company.

Is she well-groomed? Friendly? Does she communicate well? Is she obviously interested in what you have to say, or is she more concerned with telling you what she wants to say? Most important of all, do you like this person?

Remember that you will be spending a great deal of time working closely with your attorney. He or she will represent you to insurance companies and perhaps to a judge and jury. Do you feel comfortable when you imagine this person speaking on your behalf? Does the attorney instill a sense of confidence, and make you feel good about winning your case.

A successful settlement depends on successful communication between you and your attorney. If your *early* communications with an attorney don't feel "right," the *later* ones won't be a cakewalk, either!

> **You pay an attorney to work for you. You have a right to demand excellence. If you don't get it up front, you won't get it later when it really counts.**

During the initial interview, an attorney should do everything possible to put her best foot forward. If the attorney doesn't answer your questions to your satisfaction, or treats you with anything less than professional courtesy and respect, read the signals and realize that's probably as good as it's ever going to get—and walk.

If an attorney does not satisfactorily answer the first, easy questions about her professional qualifications, run—don't walk!—to the nearest exit.

Qualifying an Injury Attorney to Handle Your Case

How can you tell if an attorney who offers to handle your case is "qualified?" There are a few things that you can ask an attorney during your first meeting that will let you quickly determine whether she is truly qualified to handle your case.

Many people hesitate to ask professionals about their qualifications. Some folks fear that they may appear rude or even "nosy" if they ask qualifying questions. If you're still thinking along these lines, stop it! You need to know if an attorney can handle your case and respond efficiently to the many complex demands of a personal injury case. An attorney in general practice, or one who specializes in real estate or family law, may be an outstanding legal professional, but he probably is not the best qualified attorney to handle your personal injury case.

Think of it this way: if you needed your tonsils removed, would you go to a foot doctor?

When You Meet With an Attorney

Use the **"Qualification Checklist"** below as your evaluation
bible when you are seeking a personal injury attorney.
Don't hesitate to ask an attorney about his qualifications. A
good attorney will welcome the opportunity to discuss his
qualifications and review his personal injury experience
with you.

On the other hand, an attorney who is probably not well
prepared to handle the complexities of a personal injury case
may tend to avoid your questions, answer them in a vague
or misleading way or worst of all defensively dismiss them
altogether. Not a good sign!

If you have been seriously injured in an automobile collision,
you need to form a winning partnership with an attorney
who will be working closely with you for months or even
years. It's your responsibility and your right, to make sure that
the attorney you select to represent you has the education,
experience and ability to represent you professionally,
diligently and successfully. Only a qualified personal injury
attorney will do.

To find out if an attorney is qualified to handle your case, ask
the following questions:

Attorney Qualifications Checklist

☐ *Where did you receive your law degree?* You may not know
a law school from a beauty school, but this is a good question
to gauge the attorney's response. If he is proud of his academic
achievements at Little Wahoo U it will show. Pride in
accomplishments means pride in winning. A good sign!

☐ *Did you work in any other field before entering the field of law?* This provides you with an opportunity to find out a little bit about the background of the attorney. She may have spent five years working in the insurance industry and has a solid familiarity with the insurance business. All to your benefit!

☐ *How long have you been practicing law?* Yes, every attorney needs that first big case to cut his milk teeth. But it doesn't have to be *your* case! Experience counts in the area of personal injury. An attorney who has years of experience dealing with many different insurance companies and who is well-versed in personal injury laws is going to provide the legal representation you need to successfully settle your case.

☐ *How long have you practiced law in the State of Washington?* Personal injury laws vary from state to state. An attorney who has just established a personal injury practice in the State of Washington may not be up to speed on the intricacies of the law in our state. Her lack of experience in this state may affect your ability to gain a good settlement.

☐ *Do you specialize in certain areas of the law? Do you regularly handle personal injury cases?* What percentage of your practice is devoted to personal injury? Your best bet is finding a personal injury attorney who devotes 100% of their practice to personal injury. Anything less than 80-90% means you may not be getting the professional experience and expertise that you need to successfully settle your case.

☐ *How much trial experience do you have?* It's important to remember that your case may not settle before it goes to court. You need to have a personal injury attorney who is capable of managing the many facets of insurance company negotiation and settlement, plus the completely different set of demands and responsibilities of courtroom litigation.

☐ *To which professional associations do you belong?*
Organizational affiliations, such as the Trial Lawyers
Association, indicate a professional who is dedicated to
the law and committed to continued training and
professional development.

☐ *How long have you been with this firm? With other firms?*
An attorney who has moved from firm to firm may be very
successful and on a fast track to bigger and better things. In
the alternative, he may have been shuffled from one place to
another because of poor performance or other professional
difficulties. If there's a history of movement from firm to firm,
ask why and listen carefully to the response.

☐ *How many offices does this firm have?* A convenient
location at which you can meet with your attorney is
important, especially if you have been injured and face
transportation difficulties.

☐ *How big is your support staff?* Handling an injury claim
requires significant document management. Larger firms have
people dedicated to acquiring, organizing and providing your
medical records to your medical team of providers.

☐ *How can I contact you outside of regular office hours?*
While an attorney may not be willing to give you his or her
home telephone number, a professional attorney will provide
alternate methods (voice mail, email, answering service,
pager, beeper, cellular phone) to contact them on evenings,
weekends and holidays.

☐ *How much time do you spend in trial?* A heavy trial schedule
may mean that the attorney is not adept at negotiating
successful pretrial settlements. Also, when your attorney is in
trial on another case, she is often not available to take any
action on your case. A good attorney will inform you early
on of any upcoming trials so that you know her schedule of
availability in advance.

❏ **How much contact will be with paralegals?** It is reasonable to expect that a good PI attorney will have part of the work on your case handled by multiple staff members.

❏ **Does the legal team have a department dedicated to coordinating and disseminating medical information to your providers? Can they get all of your bills paid promptly?** Better injury firms devote resources and employees solely to this process for their clients. Avoid hiring a firm without these capabilities.

Once you have discovered some of the operational features of the attorney's practice, it's time to talk more precisely about how the attorney will help you and how much she will charge for that help.

Clarify Your Expectations

During this initial meeting, you will need to be *proactive* with the attorney. This means that you need to volunteer your own questions and concerns, and make sure that the attorney's answers satisfy you. The attorney needs to hear what you expect from him and respond with assurances that those expectations will be met.

Fees and Costs

A typical concern is, *"How much is this going to cost me?"* The amount and manner in which you pay your attorney for handling your settlement can vary from attorney to attorney. This will be covered in the Fee Agreement that you will be asked to sign if you decide to hire an attorney.

Fee Agreement

Like any other contract, you should read the Fee Agreement in its entirety. Most agreements are fairly standard and include language detailing:

◆ What the attorney will provide for you and a description of appropriate costs and payments.

◆ A description of the fee arrangement (i.e., contingency) or how the attorney is paid.

◆ What is expected of you, the client. What will be done in the event of a fee dispute.

Some Fee Agreements are a single page; others are multiple pages with tiny typed legalese. It is important that you read any Fee Agreement in its entirety and ask the attorney to explain anything you don't understand.

Contractual Obligations

The Fee Agreement is a contract that you can cancel at any time, for any reason. This means that you can fire your attorney whenever you want to and you don't even have to explain why. Keep in mind, however, that you will be obligated to pay the attorney for the work that she has put into your case. Most Fee Agreements contain language that covers payment to the attorney in the event you discontinue the representation. If you owe an attorney money for work conducted on your behalf, the attorney will typically place a lien on any settlement amount you receive and get reimbursed when your case settles.

On the other hand, an attorney may dismiss you as a client for good cause. "Good cause" is somewhat hard to prove and it is the rare attorney who will withdraw from representing you unless he has good reason to do so. If you are abusive or otherwise pose a risk to the attorney or his staff, the attorney would have good cause to withdraw from representing you. If your attorney just doesn't like you, that's not good cause.

The trick to avoiding firing and hiring attorneys (or being "fired" yourself!) is to do your homework before signing the Fee Agreement. Attorneys sell their ability to represent you. You buy that representation. It is a business partnership in every sense of the word and demands the same consideration and care you would put into forming any other business partnership. If at any time during your relationship with your attorney you are unhappy or dissatisfied, communicate with your attorney. A minor misunderstanding or miscommunication shouldn't permanently damage your working relationship. It won't if you keep the lines of communication open.

On the other hand, if you are truly dissatisfied with your attorney's representation, and your efforts to communicate go unanswered and the problems remain unresolved, it's time to move on and find representation that works for you.

Contingency Fee

Personal injury attorneys charge for their legal services on a contingency basis. This means that the attorney takes a certain percentage (usually between one-third and 40%) of the total settlement proceeds. If you do not win a settlement, the attorney does not charge a fee. Attorneys are willing to take this risk because if they do their job right and negotiate effectively, they will almost certainly be paid for their efforts.

Here is an example of a simple contingency arrangement. Your personal injury attorney has worked diligently on your case and established a high claim value. The insurance company offers to settle your case for $30,000 and writes one check in that amount made out to you and your attorney. Your attorney gets one-third, or $10,000, and you get two-thirds, or $20,000.

Contingency fees can become a little more complex. Let's say you incurred $10,000 in medical bills and your health insurance company paid all of those medical bills. In your contract with your health insurer, there is language that talks about "subrogation." This means that if your health insurance company pays for medical care you need as a result of the collision and you obtain settlement money for that collision, your health insurance company may be entitled to a partial reimbursement. This reimbursement amount may be negotiated downward by a competent personal injury lawyer.

> The difference between just another insurance settlement and a good insurance settlement is often the experienced personal injury attorney who increases the value of your claim significantly with experience, skilled negotiating abilities and a trained professional staff.

When you receive the settlement check from the at-fault driver's insurance company, your attorney will receive one-third of $30,000, or $10,000, as her contingency fee. In addition, there are probably $1,000 in costs that the attorney advanced for your case (long distance telephone charges, photocopying, copies of medical records and medical reports, etc.) So your attorney receives $11,000, and you will receive $19,000. But your medical insurer will want $10,000 of your share, leaving you with only $9,000.

But wait! A qualified personal injury attorney knows how to work with your health or PIP insurer and greatly reduce or completely cancel that $10,000 bill. And you walk away with more money in your pocket than you otherwise would have received on your own.

You may receive $15,000 by settling on your own, but an attorney may be able to settle your case for $50,000, leaving far more money for you after attorney's fees are paid. Your attorney is best qualified to determine the value of your case.

Costs

Every attorney charges for the miscellaneous costs that are incurred for handling your case. These costs may include charges for long distance telephone calls, photocopying, deliveries, depositions, medical reports, videotapes, postage, court costs, filing fees, jury fees, etc. By law, an attorney can not pay your costs for you. This could look like a shady deal offered by the attorney to hook your business and is prohibited by Rules of Professional Conduct.

Simple Advance

Different attorneys collect payment for costs in different ways. One way is for the attorney to advance your costs and be reimbursed when you settle. If your attorney manages costs this way, you will not be expected to pay anything until your case settles. This is your best option, since you are not expected to pay any cash out of your pocket until the settlement check arrives. Most attorneys who handle costs this way typically have set aside substantial funds of their own to accommodate their clients as they are going through the difficult process of recovery and settlement negotiation. This is a sign of a professional, conscientious and successful legal practice.

Advance with Interest

Be wary of this method! The attorney will pay costs as they arise, but will add an additional *finance* charge to the costs at time of settlement. This decreases the portion of settlement money that comes to you, especially if your costs are high.

Retainer

Some attorneys will ask for a retainer or a cash deposit up front and deposit that money in a trust fund. As your case proceeds, the attorney will withdraw money from the trust fund to pay costs as they are incurred. If the retainer balance is exhausted, the attorney will contact you and request that you deposit additional funds to cover impending costs. This can become a real problem for clients who do not have a steady cash flow due to injuries and employment difficulties. This may be a signal that you should look for another attorney.

Monthly Billings

Some attorneys will consolidate all of the costs for the month and issue a monthly bill to the client. The client is expected to pay the bill in full each month. This can prove to be burdensome, if not impossible, for someone who has been seriously injured in an automobile collision and is unable to work to generate income.

Direct Billing

A few attorneys will send bills for costs directly to the client as those costs are incurred. This is probably the most bothersome method for injured clients. Managing a flood of bills demanding payment can be burdensome.

Trial Costs

Trials cost money, sometimes lots of money. A trial represents a substantial investment in time and effort for the attorney. A professional personal injury attorney will discuss anticipated trial costs with you at the onset of representation. If it appears that settlement negotiations have failed and your case is going to trial, most attorneys will require that you advance anticipated trial costs before trial. This is something you must discuss with your attorney early in your case. If you are unable to afford a trial, your attorney can discuss and recommend other options, including settlement, arbitration or mediation.

Communications

Falling right behind the importance of determining "How much is this going to cost me?" come the nuts and bolts of how you're going to work with an attorney. The most important component to a successful working relationship is communication between you and your attorney.

When you first meet with an attorney, ask her to explain how the office will handle your case and how the progress of your case will be communicated to you. Some sample questions might be:

Attorney Communications Checklist

☐ How long do you think this will take to settle?

☐ What is likely to bring about settlement?

☐ If that doesn't happen, what are our options?

☐ How often and in what manner, will you be communicating with my medical practitioners?

☐ To what extent will my spouse/partner be involved?

☐ How much time will you expect of me?

☐ Should I continue speaking with my own insurance company?

☐ What kinds of telephone calls, inquiries, contacts, etc. should I refer to you?

☐ Will you call me with regular status reports? How often?

☐ Will you give me adequate advance notice of any important examinations, interviews and appearances?

☐ Will you regularly tell me what the insurance company is doing about my case?

☐ How will you notify me when the insurance company makes a settlement offer?

☐ What am I expected to do when a settlement offer comes in?

☐ Do you watch and control the costs incurred in my case?

Summary

The bad news is, finding the right attorney can be a difficult task, especially if you have been seriously injured in a collision and are undergoing a painful, protracted recovery.

The good news is, if you follow the guidelines in this chapter, do your homework, and keep an open mind and open ears, you will surely find the professional personal injury team that can provide the support, management and guidance needed to negotiate or litigate your claim successfully.

If you follow the helpful guidelines presented in this chapter and hire an attorney to represent you in your personal injury settlement, you will be assured of a productive and successful relationship with your attorney and his team.

As in all business matters, an informed consumer is a satisfied consumer. Shop carefully, and if you decide to buy, do so wisely. The financial benefits of a successful personal injury settlement are certainly worth an effort on your part to examine all of your options and get as much information as possible from as many different possible sources.

When searching for an attorney, politely avoid general practice law firms and solo attorneys. Injury law requires a competent, experienced team. A larger specialized office will have specific departments devoted to document management, hiring and coordinating medical, biomechanical and engineering experts.

The larger personal injury law firms will be able to handle all of the medical billing to the appropriate insurance companies and see that the bills are paid in full and promptly.

Insurance companies rate attorneys and law firms based on their history, effectiveness and likelihood of obtaining bigger jury awards. Personal injury attorneys all work on a contingency fee, so why not hire the very best for the same price? It costs you the same to hire your nephew fresh out of law school as it does one of the largest, best personal injury firms in Washington.

Don't shop until you drop for legal representation. Rely on your gut instinct. Do not delay or put off the decision. Immediate representation is significantly important to getting your case investigation started properly. You should find that your stress level will go down after you push all of those insurance application forms, ER bills and letters from the third-party carrier, across the desk and say: "Here you deal with all of this. I'm going to work on getting healthy."

Survival Guide *Checklist*

✓	Finding the Right Attorney
	Understand that personal injury law is a specialty. Only consider an experienced PI attorney to handle your case.
	Be proactive in your search. Look for a legal team that has a history of winning. Ask about their batting average.
	Trust your gut instinct when deciding to add an attorney to your team.
	Only meet with an attorney whose initial interview is free. Engage a firm that requires no money up front.
	Put in the time and effort in the beginning to establish a good working relationship with your attorney.
	Hire a law firm with a department dedicated to disseminating medical information to your providers and getting your bills paid promptly.
	Clarify your expectations and begin relying on your attorney for sound, experienced advice.

MANAGING YOUR MEDICAL CARE

Selecting your medical team and managing your care will play a significant role in your physical recovery. It's helpful to find a physician who will oversee the progress of your case and recovery. Remember though, that it is you who must assume primary responsibility for your recuperation and recovery. Your primary concern should always be your physical recovery.

It is important to balance your physical recovery with the time and effort necessary to deal with the financial management of your recovery. When you have accomplished this balance, you will be able to work effectively with your legal team to return to your previous financial condition. If you find that you are unable to manage the complexities of your health care, you should hire an attorney to assume the comprehensive management of all aspects of your case, including your physical and financial recovery.

Making Your Way Through the Medical Maze

If you were injured in an automobile collision, you were most likely transported by ambulance to an Emergency Room (ER). Standard procedure in the ER involves quickly diagnosing your injuries, determining whether you are facing a life threatening condition and giving treatment as required. You may have been admitted to the hospital under the direct care of a hospital physician or discharged with appropriate referrals for follow-up care by other medical caregivers.

When you were released from the hospital, you probably got a diagnosis of your injuries. You may also have been given medication or prosthetic devices, such as a soft leg splint or cervical collar, to alleviate the pain and discomfort of your injuries. The ER physician may have also provided a referral to an appropriate medical specialist for follow-up care. If you already have a relationship with a different medical caregiver with whom you wish to seek follow-up care, the ER physician will direct you to that doctor. In either case, it's important to follow-up on the referral and make an appointment for a full examination immediately.

Failure to obtain medical treatment and documentation of your injuries immediately following an injury can seriously hurt your settlement efforts.

If you experience continued pain, bruising, swelling, inability to move, headaches, nausea or other worrisome symptoms, or if you suspect that you have injuries that were not diagnosed during your initial visit to the ER before you are able to keep your appointment with the doctor to whom you have been referred, return to the ER immediately for follow up care.

Follow-up Care

Make an appointment immediately to see either the doctor referred by the ER or your personal physician. Some people are comfortable seeing a new doctor recommended by the ER physician. Others are more at ease seeing a doctor they have seen before. In any case, the important thing is to follow-up now. If you wait days, weeks or months to seek treatment for injuries received in an automobile collision, you may endanger your health. The chances of being able to prove that the injuries were caused by the collision grow more remote as time passes.

During your initial visit, your physician or Chiropractor should interview you thoroughly about the collision and your injuries. He should also review the ER records and X-rays, perform a full examination, provide appropriate diagnoses and prescribe treatment. This may include a prescription for anti-inflammatory medication, pain medication or muscle relaxants. The doctor may also recommend a cervical collar or other supporting device if the hospital hadn't already.

In many cases your family doctor will refer you to another specialist for additional follow-up care. In all cases, take your examining physician's advice and recommendations seriously and act on them. When, six months later, the insurance adjuster casually asks you why you never went to physical therapy as prescribed by your doctor, you'll know then that you just blew a large part of your settlement claim. You also likely jeopardized your physical recovery.

If your doctor doesn't offer one, ask for a treatment time line. That is, your doctor may prescribe ten visits to a physical therapist for treatment of your neck and back injuries and pain. Your Chiropractor may decide that a two month series of Chiropractic treatments are in order to fully treat your injuries.

Treatment plans should be communicated to the insurance adjuster so that the insurance company can anticipate and set aside anticipated payments, or reserves, for your settlement. The insurance adjuster will be able to properly set the reserves for settlement if he is kept continually informed of your treatment, especially important if your doctor extends or changes the treatment plan.

What if I'm Not Recovering?

If, after the prescribed term of treatment you have not reached anticipated recovery, it's time to discuss the situation with your health care provider. Is more of this type of treatment required? Should you consider alternative treatments? Is there something you should be doing that you haven't been doing to hasten recovery? Is there something else going on here, perhaps an undiagnosed injury that may be interfering with your recovery under this treatment plan? These are all issues you should discuss with your health care provider.

Communicating your concerns and desire for full recovery with your treatment provider will encourage open discussion of your situation and the options that are available to you. Usually, your treatment provider will be enthusiastic about redesigning an appropriate plan of treatment for you. It might be that a different approach to physical therapy is in order. Alternatively, he may refer you to another specialist for a second opinion and an opportunity to evaluate and modify your current treatment plan.

The worst case scenario would be your doctor shrugging his shoulders and saying, "I don't know what to do." If this happens, you need to take the initiative and suggest that you see another specialist who may have an alternative treatment plan that will hasten your recovery. Your primary goal must be full physical recovery. If you are not getting that with your present treatment provider within a reasonable period of time, it's time for you to be proactive and seek alternatives.

Some people become comfortable with one doctor. Perhaps they've been seeing this particular doctor forever and hesitate to make a change. Maybe the patient is afraid of insulting the doctor by asking to see someone else for a second opinion. As in the field of law, doctors specialize in different areas of practice. No matter how much you trust him, it doesn't make any sense to continue to see your gynecologist for treatment of a back injury.

Nor does it make much sense to continue to see a doctor who has not been able to provide successful treatment of your injuries. This can happen if your particular injury and treatment needs fall outside your doctor's specialty area. In this situation, your doctor should refer you to a specialist who has more experience with your type of injury.

If you make the decision to seek alternate treatment of your injuries, communicate your decision to your doctor and reach a mutual decision about the referral. Once a doctor has participated in your plan for recovery, you want to keep that doctor on your medical team until you have reached maximum medical improvement (MMI) and have successfully settled your claim. Even after the doctor has stopped treating your injuries, you may need to return to that doctor later for other treatment or referrals. Also, you may need to ask that doctor for medical records or testimony for your settlement claim.

Direct, clear communications are going to make any treatment changes or decisions a successful team effort between you and your medical caregiver. Coming out of the blue with a spontaneous demand that you see another doctor will likely surprise and possibly alienate your medical caregiver. Open communications can prevent detrimental surprises.

Don't Shop Until You Drop!

There's a big difference between seeking the most appropriate care and shopping indiscriminately for a doctor, any doctor. This may later look like you were on the hunt for a doctor who would provide an inflated diagnosis of your injuries and support a higher value for your claim. Seeking appropriate care is a legitimate and justifiable effort on your part to manage optimal recovery. Indiscriminate doctor shopping is fraud!

Medical, legal and insurance professionals are experts at identifying claimants who are trying to work the system for financial gain. You'll be wasting the valuable time of everyone involved and you'll irretrievably damage your case if your actions represent anything less than total commitment to finding the right medical care. Appropriate care will provide the best chances of recovery from your injuries.

Your medical history should display a conscientious effort to seek out and employ the services of medical professionals who can assist you in reaching maximum recovery. Diligently follow prescribed treatment plans before making any changes. Your record will clearly show that your treatment plan was in the best interests of your physical recovery and was not designed to abuse the system for financial recovery.

Worse yet, if your medical history shows a wide range of unrelated, inconsistent complaints to different doctors at different times or if there is no verifiable medical proof to back up your claims, your demand for settlement may appear suspect and be summarily refused by the insurance company. Professional personal injury attorneys are likely to decline to represent clients who doctor shop because they suggest either a poorly documented and losing case or an attempt to commit insurance fraud.

It is your right and your responsibility to seek out the best possible care and treatment, even if it means seeing many doctors. Try to avoid accumulating a medical history that shows that you have jumped from one doctor to another or from one form of treatment to another, without any commitment on your part to follow prescribed treatment plans and truly seek recovery. Your claim will become suspect and immediately diminish.

Your records need to show and your physical condition should demonstrate, that all of the treatment by all of the providers was reasonable and necessary. Reasonable means that the treatment was provided for an appropriate amount of time and cost; necessary means that the treatment was recommended and monitored by the attending physician. Without adequate proof of these two qualifying conditions, a long shopping list of medical treatment may be successfully refuted by the insurance company or its lawyers.

Managing Your Recovery

With a perfect mix of caring and conscientious healthcare caregivers and your executive management skills, you may have little to worry about when it comes to managing your physical and financial recovery.

However, in the real world, doctors specializing in different areas of practice don't customarily communicate with each other about your care. The truth is, your dentist has little incentive to regularly call your Chiropractor for periodic updates on your recovery. And when you're trying to coordinate a variety of appointments from one end of town to the other, mustering all of the appropriate medical records, paying the bills, calling the insurance company, struggling to return to work full time and doing all of this on crutches, your skillful management of both your physical recovery and your financial recovery may prove elusive or impossible.

> If you choose to hire an attorney to assist you in managing your full recovery, your attorney will assume the most important duties of managing your medical care. Many people injured in an automobile collision find it difficult to assume full responsibility for medical care management. If you find that you are unable to competently or comfortably manage your health care, you should hire an attorney to assume the comprehensive management of all aspects of your case, including your physical and financial recovery.

You are the best and only judge of whether or not you are up to the task. If you feel that you are, and you're not experiencing increased stress or frustration that hampers your physical recovery, then you are a good candidate for managing your own case. If, however, you have doubts about your ability to adequately manage both your physical and financial recovery, or if your are seriously injured and the time and effort needed to do it well is exacting a heavy toll on your recovery, it's time to ask for professional help.

Communicating with Your Medical Caregivers

Whether you are seeing your family doctor, a referred caregiver or an ER physician for treatment of your injuries, you need to communicate clearly and consistently with each doctor about your injuries and the effects those injuries have on your physical well-being.

Your first communication with a doctor should include a thorough and detailed description of your injuries, including how you received them and what their impact has been on you. You should discuss the effects of those injuries on your health, your expectations for physical recovery and your responsibilities in the treatment plan. Full disclosure of everything about your injuries is very important at the onset. The treatment plan prescribed by the doctor at this point will depend a great deal on what you communicate during your first visit. It is important to discuss the following with your health care providers:

Health Care Provider Communications Checklist

☐ Can you treat my injuries and what treatment do you advise?

☐ Is there anything I shouldn't be doing during treatment (lifting, working, running)?

☐ How long should my treatment continue?

☐ What happens if treatment doesn't work? Is surgery an option?

☐ Will you refer me to another doctor if necessary?

☐ Will I fully recover from my injuries? If not, what will my limitations be?

☐ What must I do to fully participate in my treatment plan now?

☐ What might I need to do in the future to continue treating this injury?

☐ Will you be available to work with me (and my attorney) in my settlement negotiations?

Managing Your Medical Records

At every step of your physical recovery, your communications with your attending physicians will most likely make their way into the medical charts. These charts become the official record of the effects of your injury, the care given to treat your injury and your recovery from the injury.

During settlement negotiations with the insurance company, the medical charts and records that your doctors create provide the foundation both for your claim and the insurance company's defense. If your injuries and their impact on you are officially noted in your medical records, there is sound evidence to prove your claim of injury, pain and suffering. This works to your advantage.

However, if you submit a claim for injuries that are not noted anywhere in the medical records, or if your own claims and assertions differ from the observations, diagnoses and treatments recorded by your medical caregivers, the insurance company will move quickly to dismiss those claims.

Every time you speak to a medical caregiver, you should provide a full and candid explanation of your injuries and how those injuries have affected you. Without proof of injury, pain and suffering evidenced by official medical records, you may well be left without any evidence to support your claims.

Ongoing communications with the insurance adjuster are also important. Your regular and comprehensive reports of your physical and financial condition document the extent and severity of the injuries and the pain and suffering you are experiencing as a result. Your reports also keep the insurance company informed on a timely basis about the nature of your injuries and your anticipated recovery from them. Remember, if you are unable to communicate in a timely manner with all insurance companies during your physical recovery and you have significant injuries, hire the best personal injury lawyer you can.

Involving the Whole Medical Team

Having said this, does it make sense to tell your dentist about the headaches you've been experiencing each morning? Yes! Your dentist has the professional experience and training to assist with a diagnosis of injury to your jaw and the surrounding tissues that may have been caused by trauma to your head, neck or back in the automobile collision. In this case, she would probably make a referral to an appropriate physician for follow-up care.

Should you tell your Chiropractor about the grinding noise in your left knee that suddenly appeared a few days after the collision? Definitely! While you may be seeing your Chiropractor for treatment of your head, neck and back injuries, he is an expert on the mechanics of how the impact of an automobile collision can cause trauma to many different parts of the body. The grinding in your knee may well have been caused by extending your leg to slam the brake pedal at the moment when you collided with thousands of pounds of high speed metal. Such tremendous forces can cause serious injury to your knee and other parts of your body as well.

The information contained in your medical records is one of the most important components of the total documentation package that will be used to support your settlement claim. Everything matters.

When you return to the neurologist for a follow-up appointment one month after your original appointment with her, is it really necessary to again recite the entire litany of your injuries and the pain, problems and limitations you have been experiencing? Absolutely! You can't communicate too much to your medical caregivers. Something that may not have found its way onto your medical chart during one appointment can always be added to your records by your doctor during a later appointment.

Keep in mind, also, that the typical medical practitioner may have hundreds, if not thousands, of other patients with their own medical histories and complaints. It's simply too much to expect that a doctor will remember your entire history each time he steps into the examining room to see you. The doctor's demanding appointment schedule may allow only a cursory review of the medical records contained in your chart. It's up to you to fill in the blanks and make sure that everything about your injuries and your recovery is communicated to your doctor and included in your medical records. This is important if you and your attorney, together, are to successfully manage your injury and treatment.

Managing Multiple Caregivers

The more extensive your injuries, the more likely you will be seeing multiple medical caregivers. You will be referred to doctors who specialize in the particular area in which you have been injured. For example, you may be referred to an orthopedist for a fractured tibia, a dentist for broken teeth, a neurologist for a closed head injury and concussion, a Chiropractor for neck and back sprain and a psychotherapist for treatment of post-traumatic stress and depression.

In this incredible mix of specialties, you may feel that your body is composed of mutually exclusive territories, where one doctor may venture for diagnosis and treatment, but where another won't dare to tread. Throughout your medical care, however, you need to remember that your body and health are combined into one comprehensive, albeit complex unit.

While it may seem that the various doctors have exclusive rights to your various bits and pieces, you are the manager of the whole business, and it's your responsibility to make sure that everyone, from Chiropractor to psychotherapist, understands the nature of all of your injuries.

The healing of your body and your mind is a team effort between all of your medical caregivers. The more medical providers you have, the better it would be to hire an experienced personal injury attorney.

When you communicate well with all of your caregivers, you are in effect giving each of them the opportunity to apply their wide ranging experience and skill to your full recovery. If you limit your communications and share only part of your injury history with some of the doctors, your whole medical team suffers for lack of complete information and total understanding of your condition.

When it comes time for your attorney to settle your case, if your medical records show that you have consistently and clearly communicated to your attending physicians about your injuries and their impact on you, and your caregivers in turn have responded appropriately with diagnoses and treatment, the value of your case is increased dramatically. On the other hand, nonexistent or incomplete medical records mean that your injuries and the value of your case can be misinterpreted by the insurance company. If there are any uncertainties about your claim, insurance companies are not very likely to give you the benefit of the doubt!

Traditional vs. Alternative Medical Care

America is now home to some of the most progressive and technologically superior medical care available in the world. It is not unusual for a seriously injured person to receive professional care from a medical team composed of an emergency room physician, a family doctor, a psychiatrist, a radiologist, a Chiropractor, a hypnotherapist and an acupuncturist. As the demand for a variety of successful treatment options continues to grow, it's becoming more and more common to find that traditional medical care shares clinic space with alternative forms of medicine.

Chiropractic

More and more people are opting for less traditional modes of medical care. Some people still think of Chiropractic as a nontraditional method of medical care. However Chiropractic has grown in popularity and acceptance among patients and traditional medical practitioners alike.

Some Chiropractors will treat only neck and back problems and injuries, and some people continue to see their Chiropractor for these reasons only. Many more people, however, view their Chiropractor as their primary health provider. These Chiropractors provide comprehensive physical care for their patients beyond the treatment of back and neck problems and injuries.

Many people prefer Chiropractic over more traditional medical care because by its very nature, Chiropractic is more of a "hands on" method of health care. The Chiropractor will manually touch, massage and manipulate your spine and related muscles and tissues to achieve maximum alignment and healthy interaction. Chiropractors tend to look at the whole picture and treat your symptoms based on a larger view of what is going on with your body and overall health. Chiropractors are not licensed to dispense prescription medications, and many patients prefer this more natural approach to healing. On the other hand, your Chiropractor will refer you to a medical practitioner in the event he diagnoses a condition for which you require treatment or medications outside of the scope of Chiropractic.

Medical reports generated by your Chiropractor are considered by the insurance adjuster as an important part of your overall medical history. Records of your care submitted by your Chiropractor are customarily extensive, detailed and comprehensive. They are a valuable part of your settlement package and will speak clearly about the neck, back and other injuries you received in the automobile collision.

Whether you choose to include your Chiropractor on your medical team for treatment of your neck and back injuries only, or if you decide to have your Chiropractor provide comprehensive medical care and act as your primary physician, it's important to incorporate your Chiropractic care with all of your other medical treatments. Your neurologist will probably not make a direct referral to a Chiropractor, because there is little cross practice interaction between the two professions, though this is increasing. That is why you need to take the initiative and ask your attending physician to invite your Chiropractor onto your team of medical providers and make him an active participant in your total recovery.

Holistic Alternatives

Other alternative methods may include acupuncture, naturopaths, herbal remedies, homeopathic treatment and massage therapy. While your treatment provider may not spontaneously refer you to one of these alternative specialties, do not hesitate to suggest these treatments as reasonable alternatives to a traditional treatment plan.

If you have knowledge of the effectiveness of an alternative form of medicine and communicate a sincere desire to apply it to your physical recovery, your treatment provider will most likely agree with your suggested plan of action. Your doctor may not give an enthusiastic blessing to this new treatment plan, but it is unlikely that a doctor who is truly concerned with your recovery will obstruct your commitment to find healing treatment, wherever your search may lead.

> Your health insurance plan may not cover some alternative medical treatments. However, if you are able to prove at the time of settlement that alternative treatments provided relief and aided in your physical recovery, you will most likely be able to receive reimbursement for such treatments as a part of your settlement. Insurance companies should provide reimbursement for all medical care that is reasonable and necessary.

If you decide to seek alternative care, make sure that you communicate your desire to your attending physician so that his agreement with your decision is noted in the medical records. Also, make sure that you report the outcome of the alternative treatment to your attending physician, especially if it is positive. A report from an herbalist will probably not be included in the official medical records used by the insurance company to assess your claim. However, your attending physician's reference in your medical chart to successful treatment by the herbalist is a valuable component of your overall medical record.

Agreeing to a settlement before you know your final physical outcome is a tremendous risk.

Maximum Medical Improvement (MMI)

It's important to reach maximum medical improvement (MMI) before settling your claim with the insurance company. MMI is achieved when your physical condition is fixed and stable. Treatment may be available that provides temporary relief, but a finding of MMI means that there is no treatment available that will permanently change or improve your condition at that point.

Why should you wait until you have reached MMI before settling? Following injury in an automobile collision any number of things can occur. You may find that two weeks after the collision, you have no lasting injuries or problems from the injury, and your physician declares full recovery. If so, celebrate your marvelous good fortune and rest assured that your claim will most likely be settled quickly. Alternatively, you may find that two years after the collision you are still unable to work or function at the level you could before the collision. Time is the great equalizer of injuries suffered in a collision. It is only after a sufficient amount of time, with appropriate treatment of your injuries and careful monitoring of your recovery, that you will have a clear idea of how serious and perhaps how permanently disabling your injuries may be.

When you're overwhelmed with pain and disability, medical bills, insurance forms to fill out, phone calls to return, unemployment worries and all the other things that seem to pile up after an automobile collision, it's really tempting to jump at a chance for early settlement. The insurance companies know (and conduct a large part of their business based on this knowledge) that the typical claimant will just want to get the whole settlement process over with and settle quickly. But until you have fully recovered, a hasty settlement is the worst possible thing you can do.

Until your medical team provides you with a final determination of your medical prognosis, you have absolutely no way of knowing when or even if your injuries will fully heal. There's no way to know if or when you will return to the condition you were in before the collision.

The more serious the injuries, the more important it is to wait until you reach MMI before considering a settlement with the insurance company. If an extended wait is causing financial hardship, damage to your quality of life, mental or emotional difficulties or just plain wearing you down, it's time to get an attorney on your side who will help you back onto the right track of physical and financial recovery. The more serious the injuries, the more you need an attorney.

Let's say you settle for $15,000 three months after the collision for head, neck, and back injuries. As a condition of the early settlement you sign a release that exempts the insurance company from any further obligation to pay for medical care incurred because of the collision.

Imagine this frightening scenario: Four months after the collision, your arms begin growing numb. The next day, you are in the hospital for major emergency surgery to remove disk fragments and repair damaged nerves in your neck. Five months after the collision, you are undergoing intensive rehabilitation for your partial and permanent paralysis.

Your world just caved in on you. Where are you going to look for payment of thousands of dollars in medical bills? Who is going to support your family? Who is going to reimburse you for the loss of your ability to walk, run, play and work? The answer: Nobody. If you settle too early, before obtaining a complete analysis and determination of your physical health and recovery, you've burned any bridge between you and full financial recovery. The results could be disastrous for your life and for your family's future as well.

Your physical recovery is the most important aspect of any insurance settlement claim.

Don't compromise your physical recovery by the temptation of an early settlement. Trust your medical team to provide the best possible care and make the most professional and educated determinations of your physical status. Don't be left holding a bag of woefully insignificant cash if your recovery falters. The quality of your life and your financial future may be damaged beyond recovery by an early, insufficient settlement.

Your medical team has the experience and expertise to determine your physical status and the prognosis, or medical prediction, of full recovery at any phase during your recuperation. The insurance companies are highly skilled at interpreting the medical reports to make an assessment of the value of your claim based on the medical prognosis. And somewhere in between, you (or your attorney) assume the full responsibility for translating the medical prognosis into a reasonable settlement for your injuries, pain and suffering.

Being the Good Patient

Developing the "good patient" in yourself is almost as important as finding good medical caregivers and developing them into a successful medical care giving team. There are a few characteristics that you'll need to develop if you want to create the most productive and successful relationship with your medical team.

Attitude

Believe that you'll recover. Don't climb up on the treadmill muttering to yourself, "This isn't going to work." And if you need psychological help to reach this belief, get it.

Discipline

Follow the treatment plan prescribed by your doctor to the letter and for as long as the doctor has prescribed it. If the doctor says no tennis, then put the racket away. If the doctor says walk a mile every day, then pull out those walking shoes and start moving.

Commitment

When you and your medical team have designed your treatment plan, commit to it with all the physical, mental and emotional resources you have. Set a recovery goal and stick to it. Ask your family and friends for their support. Prepare for the ups and downs of your recovery and don't let minor, or even major setbacks steer you off course. If you find that your commitment is wavering, get a professional coach (your attorney) to help you.

Be your own best friend during recovery. Follow the plan, work with it and make it work *for* you.

Consistency

The worst thing you can do to your health as you're recovering from your auto collision is to jump on the recovery trampoline. Saturday you feel better than you ever have since the collision, so you corral the dog and go on a ten mile uphill climb. Sunday, you can't get out of bed because you've strained your lower back again. You spend the next two weeks in intensive physical therapy, right back on square one.

Balance

This is probably the most elusive and challenging characteristic. You need to balance your life with your treatment plan. Your life probably already includes family, work, friends, social commitments and civic responsibilities. Add to this mix the complex settlement negotiations with an insurance company. If you can't balance the whole picture, you're going to lose a lot of focus. If you can't balance everything, you need help and need to hire an experienced PI attorney.

Summary

Just when you thought the insurance industry was a scary place to be, you've now entered the medical zone! Yes, it can be frustrating and frightening and sometimes a little bit painful. But when you work together and consistently communicate with your medical caregivers to design a treatment plan, and you commit yourself to that plan and set your sights on full physical recovery, you'll be amazed at the results that at first you may have thought would be impossible.

Achieving physical and financial recovery is the ultimate balancing act. At a time when your physical and financial resources may be at their lowest possible level, you will be called upon to devote increasing time, effort and expense to manage your insurance settlement claim. If you were seriously injured, hire an attorney early. Relieve yourself of the burden of attempting to juggle all the requirements of achieving both physical and financial recovery on your own.

The key word here is **team**: everyone is involved in the job of getting you back to where you were before the collision. The only way to make that team work to its fullest potential is to manage it carefully, diligently and skillfully. It's your responsibility to make sure that team management stays on track. If you are unable or unwilling to put the time and effort into managing your team, then your physical, emotional, mental and financial survival depends on your hiring someone to step in and do it for you.

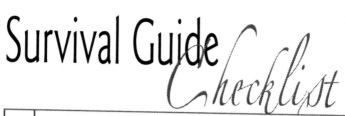

Survival Guide Checklist

✓	Managing Your Medical Care
	Determine if your attending physician will become the lead provider.
	Build a medical team with your attorney's guidance.
	Coordinate your treatment and diagnostic testing with your insurance benefits. Make sure all your bills are paid by PIP.
	Remember that your physical recovery must be your top priority.
	Be a good patient.
	If not improving, seek alternate care.
	Be involved in the management of multiple providers. Participate with your medical team to insure full physical and financial recovery.
	Ask family and friends for their help and support.
	Don't consider settlement until you have reached MMI.

PROVING LONGLASTING IMPACTS FROM AN ACCIDENT

We talked earlier in this book about managing the treatment for your injuries. Physical pain, mental exhaustion, emotional stress and the financial setbacks of recovery and recuperation shouldn't stop you and your attorney from conducting negotiations to obtain maximum financial compensation for your losses.

In this chapter, we'll talk about how mental and emotional challenges, combined with employment and financial issues, impact your life after an automobile collision. Be sure to take the time to go through all four checklists and identify each point that pertains to you. We'll review how to document these effects on your life so that your legal team can incorporate this information into a successful settlement.

The True Impact of an Automobile Collision

Few are the lucky ones who survive an automobile collision without any injuries. The potential for injury, even when automobiles collide at relatively low speeds, means that the risk of being injured in an automobile collision is fairly high. Insurance industry statistics say that the average American will be in an automobile collision once every seven years.

If this is true, why aren't there millions of people demanding insurance settlements on any given day? The number of people who even initiate a claim for an insurance settlement is only a fraction of the actual number of people injured in automobile collisions. The number of folks who successfully negotiate insurance settlements that fairly compensate them for all of their losses is an even smaller fraction of those initiating claims in the first place.

So what's going on here? Could it be that people are being miraculously healed of their automobile collision injuries? Or are insurance companies gladly and quickly paying collision victims full compensation for all of their losses, generously saving everyone the hassle and anxiety of filing a claim and pursuing settlement negotiations? Or could there be some other force at work here?

The explanation for this imbalance between the large number of people who are injured in automobile collisions and the much smaller number of people who pursue and receive equitable insurance settlements is simple. Most people who are injured do not have the physical, mental and emotional strength to successfully battle the insurance giants. Some give up immediately and decide not to even bother filing a claim with the insurance company. Others decide to negotiate a settlement, but are quickly worn down and burned out early in the negotiations by a combination of their injuries and the insurance company experts who know just where to apply the pressure to obtain early and minimal settlement.

If you've already committed to a well managed plan of successful treatment and have partnered with a legal team, then you are precisely the person who can benefit most from the information contained in this chapter. Some attention paid now to maintaining your physical, emotional and mental strength is going to payoff in the long run. You owe it to yourself to learn how you can best protect your existing personal resources. Now is the time to reinforce and rebuild your total health to reach full physical and financial recovery in the future.

Physical Injuries

Following an automobile collision, physical injuries can take many forms. Broken bones, bruises and lacerations are usually immediately visible either to the naked eye or from imaging technology like X-rays or MRI. These visible injuries can be clearly documented by your medical and legal teams and often prove to be the most treatable kinds of injuries. They are the most easily identified injuries and are readily accessible and responsive to treatment plans.

Less obvious and quite often more difficult to treat are the invisible injuries, especially soft tissue injuries that may not be evidenced by irrefutable, tangible proof. A sprained muscle, torn ligaments, cervical strain and some closed head injuries are examples of serious physical damage to your body that can be difficult to quickly diagnose or document with the kind of obvious, graphic proof that can be provided for a broken leg.

> Often it's not until several hours or, sometimes, several days after the collision that the debilitating effects of some injuries make themselves known. They often make themselves known with severe pain, impaired mobility and disability.

Automobile collisions often result in soft tissue injuries. The exaggerated twisting, jerking and distortion of your head, neck and spine upon sudden impact causes tremendous forces to act on the delicate neuromuscular system that supports your body's structural framework. Immediately after the collision, the shock and sudden jolt of adrenaline into your system may keep you from immediately feeling the effects of this incredible assault on your body.

Injuries to the Head and Brain

Injuries to the head, spine or neck can disrupt and damage the fragile neurological system that controls all of your bodily activities and functions. The same traumatic stresses that can seriously injure your neck, spine or other parts of your body can also induce serious injuries to the head and brain. Sometimes injuries to the head are obvious because of bruises, cuts or fractures of the face or skull. Other injuries to the head area may not be immediately visible at the time of the collision. Bruising, swelling, bleeding or tearing of the brain and related membranes may not be evident at first.

These injuries can cause extremely serious and debilitating symptoms that can have a profound effect on the quality of your life after an automobile collision. Injuries to the head and brain require immediate and intense treatment and ongoing care to ensure maximum recovery. Medical science is discovering that even seemingly minor injuries to the head and brain can result in permanent disability. Following an automobile collision, the ER physician performs a minimal examination to identify, diagnose and treat any life threatening head injuries. As with other sometimes invisible injuries, trauma to the head sometimes goes undetected until some time after the injury causing collision.

A head injury may seriously compromise your ability to successfully manage your settlement negotiations. If your doctor has diagnosed a head injury, consult a personal injury attorney immediately to adequately represent you and manage your settlement negotiations for you.

Injuries to other parts of the brain can affect cognitive or thinking abilities. Your ability to think about many things at once or to compute complex reasoning problems, or to remember how to perform certain tasks, may be affected by these injuries. People who receive even a minor head injury will often be disoriented for a period of time after the injury. Your doctor will determine if the disorientation is temporary, perhaps because of a concussion, or if it is more serious and requires continued treatment.

Specific brain injuries may also result in problems with muscular coordination, vision, speech or your senses of taste, smell and touch. The brain is an extraordinarily complex organ, and only a qualified specialist can adequately diagnose and treat a brain injury.

If you or your primary physician suspect any type of head injury, it is extremely important to see a specialist immediately for further diagnosis and treatment. Head injuries, especially if left undiagnosed and untreated, can create frustrating and sometimes permanent disabilities that may demand significant financial resources for a lifetime.

The complexities, confusion and frustration that often accompany insurance settlement negotiations are expected, though unfortunate, elements of the whole insurance claim process. If you're feeling overwhelmed by these new responsibilities and duties, don't assume that it's a symptom of an as yet undiagnosed head injury! Talk to your doctor about your situation, and ask your doctor to suggest ways to identify the source of your difficulties and improve your ability to function.

The Other Side of Physical Injury: Depression

A well managed medical team provides the most comprehensive rehabilitative treatment available. Working in conjunction with them, you will likely achieve MMI as targeted. But until you do reach full recovery, you will, in all likelihood, experience some negative physical effects from the injury. Often, these physical disabilities, whether temporary or permanent, are accompanied by emotional trauma as well.

Emotional distress or depression can be clearly linked to an earlier physical injury. If you're injured in an automobile collision, you may face temporary or permanent physical pain and disability. You may be unable to work for an extended period of time. Your family's daily lifestyle and financial position is suddenly disrupted and may be changed forever. Let's face it: being in a bad automobile collision is a scary experience. It's not unusual for collision survivors to have upsetting nightmares about the collision, or even experience distressingly vivid flashbacks during waking hours.

Stressful and debilitating emotional repercussions from an automobile collision can range from a simple reluctance to drive an automobile in heavy traffic to an abject terror of leaving the house at all for fear of further injury or disability. Compounding these stresses are the added pressures of managing your medical care, paying your medical bills, maintaining a progressive treatment plan, deflecting financial disaster and negotiating an insurance settlement.

> **Studies have determined that depression may be caused by emotional, mental and physical stress or trauma. If a diagnosis of depression is made by a qualified physician, it is important to communicate this with all of the members of your medical team so that all aspects of your treatment plan can adequately address this condition.**

Some automobile collision victims are so traumatized by their painful experience that they find themselves shutting down emotionally. They become unable to handle the simplest day-to-day tasks. Taking out the garbage, frying an egg for breakfast or even just walking the dog can be the daily obligation that sends you right over the stress threshold and marks the onset of emotional trauma and depression after the accident.

How Do I Know if I'm Depressed?

The nature of depressive illness takes many forms. The information contained in this section is not intended in any way to provide a comprehensive discussion of depression or other emotional responses to the trauma of an automobile collision. The checklist provided below is intended to help you decide if you need professional treatment.

If you answer "yes" to any of the questions below, consult your primary physician immediately and seek referral to a qualified mental health professional who can devise a treatment plan with you.

Radical mood swings can also be caused by severe depression resulting from physical injury. Physical injuries are treated differently than depression. It's important to seek and receive appropriate medical diagnosis and care to learn the cause of your changing moods.

Depression Checklist

☐ Do you find it difficult to keep your sense of humor?

☐ Do you find yourself unable to enjoy the things that you used to enjoy?

☐ Are you sleeping much less or much more than you did before the collision?

☐ Has your appetite changed noticeably since the collision? Have you gained or lost weight?

☐ Do you seem to care less about your personal appearance than before the collision?

☐ Has your consumption of alcohol or other drugs increased since the collision?

☐ Are family, friends or coworkers suggesting that you're just not the "same old you"?

☐ Are you getting short-tempered, angry or hostile with family, friends or coworkers?

☐ Do you find yourself upset or crying over minor situations or for no apparent reason?

☐ Is your work performance suffering because you just can't seem to get the job done?

- [ ] Do the simplest tasks seem impossible to do (making phone calls, grocery shopping, preparing meals, handling errands)?

- [ ] Do you find yourself thinking negative thoughts about yourself or your situation in life?

- [ ] Do you avoid family and friends, preferring to be alone?

- [ ] Do you ever think about hurting yourself or others?

If any one of the above describes how you're feeling now, seek qualified medical help today and make sure that every aspect of your recovery is included in your overall treatment plan.

The emotional injuries caused by physical trauma are real. The good news is they are also treatable. If you or your medical team suspect that the stress of your collision is causing depression or any other disabling condition, seek a referral to a qualified mental health professional immediately.

Only a qualified mental health practitioner can determine if you are at risk for or are presently suffering from depression or a related illness. Left untreated, emotional stress and depression can quickly lead to physical illness that will interfere with your ability to fully recover from your collision.

Documenting the Effects of the Collision on Your Employment

Most people injured, whether physically, mentally or emotionally, in an automobile collision are employed at the time of the collision. Some of these folks are able to return to work immediately after the collision with little or no interruption. Others are not so lucky, and face continued medical treatment and prolonged physical recovery that either limits or entirely prevents them from returning to work.

If your doctor has ordered you to limit or discontinue working, immediately provide a written copy of the doctor's order to the insurance company. This puts the insurance company on notice that you will be claiming reimbursement for lost wages. A typical physician's order will include date of the injury, nature of the injury, why you should limit or discontinue working, and the expected date of your return to part or full-time employment.

> If your doctor's orders change, either shortening or extending the limitations on your ability to work, notify the insurance company immediately.

While you are recovering from your injury, it's important to document every single minute that you are unable to work because of the injury. If you are employed, the insurance company will eventually request that your employer provide copies of your time sheets or other attendance records to verify your claims of inability to work and the resulting lost wages. Don't depend solely on your employer's records, however. Keep your own personal record of dates and times when you are unable to work because of pain, disability or attendance at medical appointments. Include copies of this record with your claim for lost wage reimbursement.

If you customarily worked a forty hour week plus ten hours of overtime each week before the collision, but are only able to work 35 hours each week after the collision, document this fact with copies of your time sheets before and after the collision. Time records indicating a 35 hour work week after the collision may not accurately reflect the fact that your ability to work overtime was reduced dramatically and your income suffered following the collision.

Provide additional written documentation other than your official time sheet that specifically references the difference between your pre and post collision total hours worked. A letter from your employer stating that before the collision you were always available and willing to work overtime, but after the collision you weren't even able to put in a 40 hour week, will more clearly support your claims for wage loss.

If You Are Self-Employed

If self-employed, documenting your damages will be more difficult. To justify the claim that your ability to work was affected by the collision, you will have to produce documentation providing sufficient proof that you worked a relatively steady number of hours or earned a consistent living during the period preceding the collision. You don't have the luxury of dropping by the company payroll department for official copies of your records. You'll be responsible for identifying, organizing and producing the documentation that verifies your employment history. If seriously injured you should hire an attorney immediately after the accident to assist in documenting your earnings loss and future losses.

No amount of insistence from you that you "planned" on getting a job soon, or "hoped" to make more money from your business or "anticipated" getting a raise were it not for the automobile collision will convince the insurance company that you suffered compensable wage loss. You must have solid, factual documentation to back up your claim.

Gather copies of contracts and agreements that you have with past, current and future clients. Project proposals, even if they didn't result in a contract agreement with a client, may be useful as well. They present a good picture of how much work you were actively soliciting and were prepared to do, and how much you would have earned from the work, had you not been limited by the collision.

If you are claiming that you were unable to complete a proposed project because of the collision, you will need to provide solid verification from your doctor stating that you were unable to physically conduct the proposed work because of your injuries. Also provide verification from the potential client stating that they would have hired you had it not been for your inability to work because of the collision.

As in most every other financial area, the self-employed face added burdens of proof and documentation. If you're self-employed, you may need the help of an attorney to counteract what may become exhaustive demands by the insurance company to prove your wage loss claims.

Ask your clients for letters verifying that you performed certain services and how much time you took to complete each project. Better yet, prepare letters for them so that all they need to do is add their signature. Invoices or billing statements from before and after the collision should also be included in your documentation to show how your income decreased after the collision. Start by providing a six-month review of your self-employment history, and be prepared to respond to such requests as they arise.

You'll need to obtain verification from your employer (or provide documentation from your own files if you're self-employed) that matches each one of your wage loss claims.

Submit copies of the Profit and Loss Statements or Business Plans that you use for financial planning to substantiate your claims of damage to your business. Refer to bank loan or line of credit applications for additional, verifiable proof of your financial status before and after the collision. Be prepared for the insurance company to ask for copies of your bank deposits to verify your income claims.

Proving Wage Loss

When you're documenting your wage loss and other employment related damages, you need to be precise about the dollar amounts that you are claiming. The only way to effectively prove your case is to provide irrefutable facts. Following are some guidelines to help determine a reasonable claim and how to support it.

Wage Loss Checklist

You must provide proof of:

- ☐ How much money you earned each pay period during the six months before the collision.

☐ How much money you earned each pay period following the collision, to date.

☐ How many hours you worked each pay period during the six months before the collision.

☐ How many hours you worked each pay period following the collision, to date.

☐ Document any anticipated raises, promotions, cost-of-living or performance based salary increases that you lost because of the collision.

☐ List all employment related benefits, reimbursements, bonuses, profit sharing, sales commissions, gifts or awards that you would have received had you continued to work at your pre-injury level.

☐ List all employment related medical, employment or other insurance benefits that you may have lost or needed to pay for out-of-pocket because of your inability to work.

☐ Provide medical records, including a copy of the doctor's order, which documents the diagnosis, dates of disability and the anticipated date of your return to work.

Documenting How the Injury Affects Your Ability to Work

How you are able to perform your work is related to, but separate from, how much you are able to earn. If you are unable to return to your old job the next issue is if your new job will pay you the same. For example, if you are a musician and crushed your hand in an accident, you probably will need to discontinue playing the piano for a living. You may be able to retrain and begin a new profession as a real estate agent.

In this case, you will need to prove that the pain and suffering of being forced to leave your beloved profession, even if the change resulted in an increased income for you, demands financial reimbursement. Your ability to succeed on these complex issues is directly related to your ability to successfully negotiate everything the insurance industry will throw in your way to make it look like you may be better off financially after losing your hand.

> Different injuries produce different results for different people. Together, you and your medical team will discover as you recover from your injury what, if any, limitations you'll be facing in the future.

If your doctor orders you to permanently limit, restrict or change your employment, the calculation of anticipated wage loss becomes extraordinarily complex. You should hire a qualified personal injury attorney to represent you and negotiate a settlement that will protect you and your family from a lifetime of financial loss.

More typical are those cases where injuries received in an automobile collision either temporarily or permanently, and partially or substantially, limit your ability to perform the work that you did before the collision. A back injury can limit you to lifting no more than five pounds, when before the collision you were lifting 80 pound packing boxes with ease. Cervical trauma can prohibit you from sitting for more than 20 minutes at your computer, where before your injury you worked four and five hour stretches without a break.

The most critical aspect of documenting how your injury affects your ability to perform your job is the medical record created by your treating physician. Your doctor isn't going to be able to record your limitations in your medical chart unless you clearly communicate those limitations during each medical examination,

If your condition improves, let your doctor know that your ability to conduct your work is also improving. However, if your injury continues to prohibit you from doing your work, you have two choices: either change your treatment plan to provide more successful treatment of the injury or change your working environment. Your treating physician is most knowledgeable about the appropriate course of action for you.

> If, at any time, your employment conditions change, whether it's short-term or long-term, notify the insurance company immediately so that they are prepared to respond to your eventual claims for related wage loss.

If your doctor orders you to change your working environment, you will need to involve your employer. Legal requirements prohibit discrimination against disabled workers. Your employer will likely respond quickly to a physician's orders to accommodate special needs required by the nature of your injury, especially if those special needs are short term. Special needs may mean a five minute break every hour to alleviate stresses on your neck, or reassignment to a job that doesn't require lifting heavy loads.

Complications arise if your doctor's orders require substantial accommodations or long-term special considerations. There are some instances where an employer simply won't be able to meet your special needs. If, for example, you are a carpenter working in a small cabinet shop, and you lose the ability to use your right arm, there may not be alternative employment opportunities at that particular business that reasonably match your reduced abilities.

In this case, your doctor will order alternative vocational training that allows you to perform work that is better suited to your diminished physical abilities.

Determining future wage loss is the process of applying complex mathematical formulas to established industry norms and statistics. If you find yourself in a situation where you are forced to change your vocation or stop working altogether, you absolutely must have representation by an attorney trained in this complex area of the law to determine your true losses.

Quality of Work Checklist

If your doctor has ordered you not to return to your previous job or has ordered you to permanently reduce or restrict employment, provide testimony and medical records documenting this. Documentation should include:

- ☐ Date of collision.

- ☐ Date employment limitations began.

- ☐ Anticipated date of return to employment.

- ☐ Why you are unable to work, detailing the specific injuries that contribute to this.

- ☐ Any restrictions against returning to your former employment.

- ☐ Specifics about the temporary or permanent nature of your disability.

- ☐ If applicable, your physician's orders to retrain or seek alternate employment.

☐ A detailed list of those functions of your job that you are unable to perform as a result of the collision. Provide medical records supporting your claims. Some functional losses may include an inability to get to work, lift, sit, stand, bend, cradle the telephone, drive, operate a computer, operate machinery or heavy equipment, stock, reach overhead, carry a sample case or other required equipment, wear required uniform or safety equipment or use common tools or perform typical office tasks (like stapling, collating, photocopying or filing).

☐ Documentation of the limitations caused by injuries that may not be related to physical movement such as memory loss, speech, sight or other sensory impairments, disfigurement or other disability that affects your ability to deal with the public or restrictions because of prescribed medication, level of energy or depression-related disabilities.

☐ A detailed list of any functions related to work and activities in which you were unable to participate as a result of the collision, such as the annual retreat, continuing education, business seminars or business promotions. Detail how your financial compensation was impacted.

Documenting How Your Injury Affects Your Quality of Life

It is just as important to document the effects of the injury on your personal life as it is to document how the collision affected your ability to work and earn a living. In fact, many collision victims find that it is in basic day-to-day living that they experience the most severe problems and difficulties as they recover from their injuries.

The best way to document how the collision has negatively impacted the quality of your life is to think about everything you do from the time you wake up until you go to sleep. Consider also all of the things you do (or used to do) outside of your home, whether taking care of personal business or pursuing your favorite hobbies. Here is a sample checklist that may help you to identify and document the many areas of your life that can be adversely affected by an injury.

Personal injury attorneys typically use a combination of effective methods to document the effects of an injury on the quality of life. Written and audio testimonies, photographs, videotapes and high-tech computerized graphics and narratives are often used to provide compelling proof of disability.

Quality of Life Checklist

☐ **Are there any limitations when you bathe, groom or dress yourself?**

For example, you have difficulty getting in and out of the bathtub, holding the hair dryer over your head causes numbness in the arm, your inability to lean over and pull on hosiery because of back spasms, dentures that don't fit because the required medication dehydrated your mouth or inability to wear high heels due to low back pain.

☐ **Has your ability to prepare meals been affected?**

For example, you can't lift dishes from overhead shelves, standing for long periods at the stove causes severe leg pains, the rotating motion of stirring ingredients causes wrist pain or loss of appetite prevents any joy of cooking.

❏ **Is your ability to maintain the household limited?**

For example, you can't push the vacuum cleaner, are unable to bend over to pick up children's toys, can't kneel to clean the floors due to a knee injury, find that continuing back pain prevents you from taking the dog for a morning walk, stiffness in your hands make doing dishes impossible or inability to maintain your garden because of limited mobility.

❏ **Are you able to manage your customary daily errands and activities?**

For example, you can't carry the shopping basket because of tenderness in elbow, are unable to load/unload groceries from the car because of back spasms or are unable to stand in line at Post Office because of swelling in injured ankles.

❏ **Are you able to transport yourself with the same degree of ease and comfort?**

For example, you are unable to drive without abject terror, opening the heavy car door causes pain in your shoulder, your doctor told you not to ride a bicycle until you get knee replacement surgery, you can't turn your neck to check for traffic, you can't take trips longer than ten minutes without extreme lower back pain, you can't take the bus anymore because you can't stand longer than five minute or you can't lift the baby out of the car seat.

❏ **Are you and your partner or family experiencing problems?**

For example, you haven't been able to go camping because of headaches, you haven't had sex in eight months due to back surgery, you quit drinking for 14 years but started again after the collision because the pain was intense, your kids are afraid to ask you to do anything because you burst into tears, your husband filed for divorce because he said that you're impossible to live with, you gained 65 pounds and your wife refuses to go anywhere with you or since you went on anti-depressant medication, you don't have the energy to do anything with your husband.

☐ **Are you having difficulties with your social relationships?**

For example, you had to resign from the Board of Directors because you just don't have the energy to perform the tasks, your bridge group won't come to your house anymore because you can't clean the house, you haven't been asked out once since you started using the cane, ever since you had to quit working, you never see your friends from work, you've gained 25 pounds and you're just too depressed to visit your friends or all your friends are into wind surfing and, since the collision, you never see them anymore.

☐ **Are you experiencing financial problems because of the collision?**

For example, you can't do the housework any more so now you have to pay $240 a month to a maid service, you couldn't plant your vegetable garden this year and now you're spending $150 more each month for produce at the grocery store, you had to cancel your family's health club membership because you can't afford it, you sold the car to buy groceries, you haven't worked for six months, the bank foreclosed on the house and you're in collections with all your creditors or you postponed getting braces for your son because you couldn't work and lost your dental coverage.

☐ **Have you noticed a personality change?**

For example, you used to have a great sense of humor, but nothing makes you laugh any more, you're so frustrated by these new physical limitations, you just cry all the time, your whole life seems like one big doctor's appointment, after 30 years in the business, now they tell you that you have to change jobs, and it scares you to death, you never felt that anything could stop you from working out and feeling healthy and strong, and now you feel like a disabled, nervous wreck, all these medications make you feel weird all day long, you used to love being around children, but you just can't handle their physical demands any more or the chronic pain makes you feel angry all the time.

☐ **Are you unable to enjoy the fun things you used to enjoy?**

For example, you can't play the piano because suspending your arms causes severe back spasms, you gave up bowling because of migraines, you can't ski because of the cervical fusion, you gave up coaching Little League because you can't manage the equipment, you lost your recreational pilot's license because of required medications, this is the first year in 30 years that you haven't planted your flower garden because of your back injury, you can't lift your 5 year old son and he keeps asking why you don't play with him any more or you had to sell your horse because your doctor told you never to ride again.

☐ **Are you having trouble sleeping?**

For example, you're always exhausted because you can't get any sleep, you sleep too much and sleep right through the alarm, you're up every two hours with back and neck pain, you're having terrible nightmares about the collision or you had to buy a new adjustable bed just so you could sleep.

Of course, your own lifestyle, habits and hobbies will dictate your personal list of how the collision injuries have affected the quality of your life. The important thing to remember is that when it comes time to prove pain, suffering and financial losses, the insurance company will want verifiable, documented proof that your life changed significantly after the collision and that those changes were directly related to the collision.

When evaluating how the injury diminished the quality of your life, the most important allies on your documentation team are your physician and your family, friends and associates. Your physician is especially important because the effects of the injury that you mention to your doctor are recorded in your medical charts and become a valuable part of the documentation trail leading to successful settlement.

Your family is a vital source of information and documentation of the debilitating effects of the collision. They are the people who see firsthand how you may have been forced to adjust your life to meet the demands and limitations of your injury and recovery. As you prepare for settlement negotiations, you will want to obtain written or recorded statements from your family that substantiate and validate your claims of pain, suffering and financial loss.

Summary

A fundamental part of participating with your legal team towards a successful settlement is providing the documentation that supports your claim. In this chapter, we talked about how automobile collision injuries can limit your physical, emotional and mental abilities. These impairments can adversely affect your job, your personal life, financial future and that of your family.

Being injured in an automobile collision is a serious and traumatic event. Those people who choose to walk away from such an experience without pursuing treatment or negotiating financial compensation for their losses may be making a mistake that will haunt them physically, emotionally and financially for the rest of their lives.

If you are suffering in any way because of your automobile collision, you first need to do everything in your power to seek appropriate medical treatment. You also need to actively pursue compensation for your ordeal. If you don't think you can do any of these things on your own, ask for help. Your family, friends, employer, doctor and your attorney can be valuable members of your team if only you communicate your needs.

We can guide you to appropriate health care, and we can direct your attention to documenting those areas where you have experienced the greatest losses. We can even recommend when to seek professional help. But in the end, you alone will make the decisions that will ultimately dictate the success or failure of your recovery on all fronts.

If you have been injured in an automobile collision, there is no reason for you to assume or expect that your damages and losses are yours to bear indefinitely without remedy or relief. Remember that you have the right to be compensated for your pain, suffering and financial losses. The law is on your side, but the responsibility for seeing that it remains there is yours alone. Your legal team will assist you by providing the necessary facts to the insurance company with organized, detailed documentation, conduct skillful negotiation of the settlement terms and confidently demand what is rightfully and reasonably yours.

Survival Guide *Checklist*

✓	*Proving Longlasting Impacts From an Accident*
	Speak up if you think you have suffered an invisible head injury.
	Know the warning signs of emotional distress and depression. Review the Depression Checklist.
	Emotional injuries require immediate treatment also. Do not delay!
	If seriously injured add a personal injury attorney to your team early.
	Document everything as it occurs to make your claim more manageable.
	Ask your employer for help when documenting the impact of the collision on your ability to work.
	Communicate the effects of the collision on your personal life.

STRATEGIES ATTORNEYS USE TO RESOLVE CASES

y life's work with thousands of injured claimants has led me to an understanding of the requirements to make this journey successfully. My law firm's team of professionals in our offices throughout Puget Sound help the injured develop a plan in each case and get it done. We solve problems.

In this chapter you'll learn the steps involved in preparing the demand. We will also give you an insider's glimpse at negotiating strategies that lead to successful resolutions. Getting a fair settlement is difficult. The more you know, the better you can participate in and appreciate the enormous amount of work that it takes. It is extremely important that you hire a qualified personal injury attorney team to help you receive adequate compensation from the at-fault party and their insurance company. Hiring an attorney does not guarantee success, but not hiring an attorney guarantees that you will fall short of your potential.

Sometimes parties find themselves in situations where settlement negotiations fail. We will review other available options, including arbitration, mediation and litigation.

Marshaling Records and Bills

From day one, it is necessary to start collecting all of your medical records and bills from every medical provider who has treated your injuries. One must also keep track of all other medical care that you received during this time, even if it is not related to your collision injuries.

If the insurance company discovers that you have withheld information about receiving medical care of any kind since the collision, they may be able to successfully claim that you purposefully withheld this information. It could be argued that other injuries or illnesses had an adverse effect on your recovery from the collision injuries and are not the other driver's fault.

What may appear to you to be unrelated medical care could actually be related to your collision injuries. It's important to gather all your medical records and have them reviewed to see if any unrelated medical treatment may in fact be related to your collision. For example, problems with your dental alignment that mysteriously show up after a rear end collision may be related to a TMJ condition contributed to by cervical sprain suffered in the collision.

List all of your care providers for your legal team. These might include an ambulance company, hospital emergency room, physical therapist, dentist, Chiropractor, massage therapist, orthopedist and X-ray facility. Hospitals often contract out to independent medical companies for diagnostic and testing procedures. Your hospital bill may reflect only partial charges. Other services may be billed to you separately.

These types of bills and records often become lost in the shuffle, especially if some time has passed after the collision. If your insurance is billed directly for your medical care, you may not actually see many of the bills. Someone will need to personally contact each provider and request an itemized statement for all services provided.

When requesting records from a care provider one needs to be sure to request the entire file. If a general request for medical records is submitted, the care provider will sometimes send only what they think you may need. The entire file might include notes, correspondence between the provider and the insurance company and miscellaneous test reports that are vitally important to your case.

There will be a charge for copies of the entire file, so it's important to work out payment details with the care providers when requesting the records. Washington law sets the standard fees that medical practitioners can charge for records. You may want to familiarize yourself with those fees.

Medical bills may also be requested from your own health insurance carrier. There is customarily no charge for this service, but the request must be in writing. When writing a request, be precise.

Apart from your medical records and bills, written narrative reports from your caregivers may also be requested. These reports should verify the nature and extent of your injuries, the required care, lifestyle changes and the likelihood of permanency and future treatment. Doctors' report charges vary, but most will require payment in advance. It's sometimes no easy task to convince a busy medical practitioner to take the time to prepare a written report, but persistence and a thoughtful prepayment for the doctor's report will usually produce results.

If you are unable to handle document management of this scope or if you can't afford the cost of requesting records and reports, you may want to refer the task to an attorney. Law office staff and resources are geared to extensive document management, and the costs of securing the documents are typically advanced by the attorney and deducted from the final settlement amount. This spares you the hardship of large out-of-pocket expenses during your negotiations.

You may want to consider reviewing all of your records with your legal team to make sure that they have an accurate, comprehensive chronology of your care. If any records or bills are missing, they can be requested from the appropriate provider. The insurance company will review your history of care thoroughly. You must have the same information they do if you're to launch successful settlement negotiations.

The records and bills are then organized by provider in chronological order, and copies are provided to the insurance company. Make sure that you also keep a copy of everything for your own records. It's not unusual to forward documents to the insurance company only to be told months down the line that they were never received or were misplaced and have to be replaced.

The records and bills that are gathered from the health care providers will provide the substance of your settlement demand package. Taking the time as they are received to organize them, in what can turn out to be hundreds of pages of records and bills, will make for more efficient and effective preparation of the demand later.

Determining the Value of Your Case

In Chapter 7, we talked about the different ways an injury can affect the quality of your life, both vocationally and avocationally. Once you have identified all the different ways in which the collision has impacted your life, you will need to work closely with your attorney to assist in determining the value of those losses.

When we ask the insurance company for a settlement that fairly compensates you for your losses, we will need to present a relatively accurate idea of the worth of the losses. You will need to specify the financial losses and how the injuries damaged your quality of life.

The determination of value rests in large part on the actual injuries suffered in the collision, along with type and duration of treatment. Insurance adjusters do not have an industry rule book to find out how much they should pay for an injury. For the most part insurance adjusters, based on their years of experience and company resources, generally have a pretty good feel for a reasonable settlement amount for a particular injury or injuries.

If you are trying to settle your own case, you are at a distinct disadvantage. You don't have years of experience and voluminous statistics upon which to base a reasonable value for your claim. If you are uncertain about what a reasonable claim value is, don't hesitate to consult with a personal injury attorney who may be able to provide you with some ballpark figures. If you have a larger claim, an insurance company is less likely to take you seriously if you are representing yourself.

While adjusters still use their personal experience and judgment when evaluating claims, many insurance companies are now using a computer program called Colossus to evaluate injury claims. Colossus determines what your claim is worth, not the adjuster. Colossus does not know you and is not able to take into consideration anything other than data from your medical records. As a general rule, when Colossus is used to evaluate a claim, the offers are usually low and do not represent fair compensation for your injuries. You should ask your adjuster if Colossus is being used to evaluate your injury claim. If Colossus is evaluating your claim, contact an experienced personal injury attorney who understands and knows how to deal with this program and the insurance companies that use it. The earlier you hire an attorney when Colossus is involved, the greater the chances for a reasonable financial recovery.

> There is no set formula or rule by which you can make a determination of loss and value. This is difficult to do. Experts in insurance and law spend years developing the ability to evaluate cases and come up with a consistent range of value for each case.

Your claim value depends on a combination of many things. Foremost in any claim valuation is the extent and severity of your injuries. If your injuries are permanent and disabling in nature, then your claim value increases provided, of course, that your care providers thoroughly document your claim. In addition to the injuries themselves, you also need to consider how those injuries have affected the quality of your life and your lifestyle. The insurance company will require extensive documentation to prove your claim that the injury curtailed your ability to live your life as you did before the collision.

The insurance company will also take into consideration other less objective facts when reviewing your claim. They'll be looking for characteristics of your claim that will assist them to assign a value on the low end of the settlement range.

What are the indicators that alert the insurance company to a lower claim value? For starters, a lack of corroborating statements from your medical providers will immediately diminish the value of your claim. Also, if you are untruthful or inconsistent in your statements, the insurance company will focus on that and greatly reduce or entirely reject your claim. Other alarms that encourage an insurance company to fight your claim are the existence of prior injuries, especially those that you failed to disclose to the insurance company early in your negotiations with them.

Determining future losses caused by a disabling injury is a difficult procedure. If you have permanently disabling injuries, you must have an experienced personal injury attorney represent you against the insurance company.

How you pursued and obtained medical treatment for your injuries is crucial in setting the value of your claim. If you did not see a doctor for treatment until long after you were originally injured, the insurance company will rightfully suspect that your injuries may not have been all that serious because they didn't warrant immediate medical attention. Gaps in your medical care are also bad news for your claim's value. If you discontinued treatment three months after the collision and then resumed treatment seven months later, the insurance company is going to decide that your lack of need for any medical care during that long period indicates that you recovered from your injuries early on. The insurance company is not going to be very responsive to your claims that many months after the collision, you've suddenly discovered that you now need medical care.

Many years of experience and statistics prove that certain injuries require certain medical care. If your medical care departs from the established standard of care, the insurance company is going to quickly suspect that you are not receiving necessary or reasonable care, and they will reject your claim.

Another reason for a low valuation or outright rejection of your claim is if you see only one provider and submit excessive medical bills, especially if you failed to obtain any relief or improvement for your injuries. A common misconception among the general public is that an insurance settlement should somehow equal three times the medical bills. This is not true. As much as we may not want to believe it, specific injuries dictate specific settlement amounts. If your specific injuries are only valued at $10,000, the insurance company is not going to provide a higher settlement amount if you pursue excessive medical care that rings up a bill of $15,000.

The insurance company will pay a settlement that fairly compensates you for your damages and losses. If you accumulate medical costs that do not accurately reflect typical care for the types of injuries that you received, the insurance company is under no obligation whatsoever to compensate you for the excessive medical charges, unless your providers clearly document the need for extraordinary care.

Legal Negotiation Strategies

When evaluating your claim for settlement, the insurance adjuster considers you as an individual in addition to your actual injuries. However, as discussed previously, if the adjuster is using Colossus, only data matters. The adjuster will only offer what Colossus allows even if he values your claim higher.

If your case fails to settle and makes its way into a courtroom, Colossus data no longer matters. The jury is going to make a determination of financial compensation based in large part on how much they like you as a person. The adjuster knows this all too well and goes back to considering you as an individual. When your profile makes a good impression, the adjuster will remember this and perhaps make more of an attempt to fairly settle your case without going to trial.

Success depends, in part, on always displaying a willingness to discuss your settlement openly and fairly and without resorting to argument, threats or abusive language. There's a big difference between being intelligently assertive and belligerently aggressive. The adjuster is not going to be very responsive to a demand for a high value if he is jumped all over and undergoes unreasonable demands in an argumentative, in your face fashion.

Gaining control early on and keeping that control is what will make or break your claim for a settlement. Confidence, clear communication and a good impression put control in your corner early on. Persistence, consistency and accurate and complete documentation keeps it there throughout the negotiations.

If you attempt to represent yourself and make a bad first impression, an adjuster is going to realize that you're not likely to succeed at trial. You can make a bad impression if you appear poorly groomed or inappropriately dressed. You're doomed if you don't have all the facts straight about your case. If you appear disorganized, disinterested or uninformed, the adjuster is going to take this as an open invitation to control the outcome of your settlement right from the beginning.

When it comes time to actively negotiate a settlement, there are a variety of strategies that PI attorneys use. Some experts believe that it's important to start high, then work down from there. Others claim that the best strategy is to determine the settlement amount wanted, start with a number in that range and stick with it.

If you are handling your own case, try to get a feel early on where the adjuster stands on negotiation strategies. If the adjuster begins your first discussion with "We'll give you $10,000 and not a penny more" and hangs up the phone, you may not have much room to negotiate. However, most adjusters are instructed by their employers to provide a settlement that rests somewhere on the low end. This means that there is actually quite a bit of room to negotiate. Many insurance adjusters are in the business because they enjoy negotiating. The ones who have been in the business for a while are darn good at it.

Get to know the adjuster personally. Conduct the negotiations on the adjuster's territory. Everyone is more likely to give concessions and cut a little more slack if they're feeling comfortable and dominant on their own turf.

Smaller dollar amounts shouldn't require excessive negotiations. If you're squabbling into the third week with the insurance adjuster over your demand for $4,000 and the insurance company's settlement offer is $3,750 and nobody's giving an inch, there's something wrong with this picture. Is it really worth your time, effort and emotional well-being to drag out a difference of only $250? At some point, pride has to give way to reason. In this case, you would probably be better off taking the $3,750 and putting the settlement negotiations behind you.

Conversely, larger dollar amounts customarily involve more extensive negotiations and a complex set of strategies. If claiming $75,000 in medical costs, an insurance adjuster is obligated to define a settlement that best represents the interests of the insurance company (keeping money in their bank account) while maintaining a good faith effort to provide a reasonable settlement (paying an amount that fairly represents compensation for losses). In a situation where the injured party's demand is in the tens of thousands of dollars, it is not unusual to see a huge gap between the demand and the offer early in the negotiations.

In every situation requiring negotiation and especially where negotiations will likely continue for a period of time, there are a few basic negotiation strategies to remember.

What's the trick to successful negotiations? It depends on what's being negotiated, who is doing the negotiations and the environment in which the negotiations are taking place.

First, remember that negotiating strategy is not just a matter of figuring out how much your case is worth. More importantly is how the legal team is going to prove the reasonableness of the claim and maximize its amount. Any claim is only as good as its proof. Marshaling records and bills, providing ample support documentation, statements from family, friends and coworkers and communicating the injured's personal experiences clearly and consistently, are only one basic aspect. There are multiple other negotiation strategies that in combination persuade an insurance company to pay more.

The value of every claim is how much an insurance company is willing to pay or how much the judge or jury is willing to award. If you choose to do this on your own without the assistance of a professional, you'll need to do research at a law library. Review the settlement amounts of cases that have gone to trial and identify those cases where the injuries closely match yours. This will provide you with a range, however settlements and awards often differ, so be careful.

Experience helps the legal team know where to start and how much to ask for. The client decides how much to settle for, with the advice and guidance of counsel. These two amounts may be significantly different. The legal team makes movement downward throughout the process, each new demand attempts to send a message as to where the final range should be. An adjuster will sense when the demands are more serious which will prompt him to respond with more reasonable counter offers.

Of course, if you are handling your own smaller claim and provide a figure early on which the insurance adjuster immediately agrees with and rushes the settlement papers to your house in thirty minutes or less, that's a clue that you probably just sold yourself short. What can you do in this case? Probably nothing. Once you give control of the negotiations to the insurance company by agreeing to a particular settlement amount, there's not much you can do to convince them to increase the amount.

Additional strategies that successful attorneys use include being persistent. A phone call each week is not excessive. "Just calling to see if you've had a chance to review my recent settlement demand." "Wanted to touch base with you to see if there's anything you needed to help you make a decision on my settlement claim." Offering to do something for the adjuster in exchange for a concession by him is an effective strategy. Ask the adjuster, "What do you need that will make it easier for you to come up to $7,000?" Also we know that action has to follow an offer. When we make an offer to make the adjuster's job easier, we follow through immediately!

Negotiating a settlement claim is just like buying a car or a house. Experts agree that the best strategy is to take all of the emotional involvement out of the negotiations. This is difficult to do when you're trying to settle your own case, especially when you're asking for compensation for your personal pain and suffering. Keep it factual, make it informational and remain objective.

Listen! The most successful negotiators learn to listen to the other party. If one is busy talking, you can't hear what the adjuster has to say about the claim. If the adjuster voices a concern about some element of the claim, we focus our attention on the adjuster's objection and put energies into identifying a solution that will overcome the objection. A good response is, "What can I do to make that more acceptable to you?" Then LISTEN to the adjuster's suggestion and take appropriate ACTION.

Negotiation is not a win or lose situation. It's a compromise. Threats, anger or accusations will not work to improving an advantage when negotiating with the insurance company. Being overly reactive, argumentative, pushy or unreasonably stubborn will offend the adjuster and turn the negotiations into a one-sided and possibly personalized battle where the adjuster will simply turn you off and refuse to budge an inch.

A personal injury professional can calculate future losses for wages, medical bills, retirement and other benefits. These calculations require technical expertise.

On the other hand, when an attorney feels that the adjuster is not responding fairly or responsibly to reasonable demands, we don't hesitate to go above the adjuster and voice concerns about the handling of the case to the supervisor. The key is doing this calmly and intelligently. Screaming at the adjuster's supervisor will only accomplish the result of encouraging two employees of the insurance company to do everything in their power to thwart a reasonable settlement.

When we find that settlement negotiations are deadlocked and nobody's moving in either direction, we take a close look and determine what's not working. We ask what we or the adjuster are doing that is stalling the negotiations? Often we sit down with the adjuster and talk frankly about the situation. We ask the adjuster for suggestions on how to bridge the gap. This is something that most people find hard to do. However, if you keep a cool head and focus on the importance of compromise rather than winning all the chips, one may find a successful resolution to the stalemate.

The best settlements result from negotiations during which the claimant's attorney becomes the adjuster's working partner. Whatever can be done to make the adjuster's job easier, and his life more pleasant, will probably be rewarded by more cooperative and conciliatory responses from the adjuster. This is not to say that you have to beg or bribe the adjuster into reaching a reasonable settlement.

If your claim is reasonable and backed up by comprehensive documentation that provides the required proof, then a cooperative and proactive approach will more likely be successful. You'll be able to overcome the standard objections and hesitations that any insurance adjuster must, by his or her job definition, apply to your claim and the final settlement value. Both of you will walk away from the negotiation table knowing that reason and fairness prevailed. That's a successful closure to any settlement negotiation.

Building an Effective Demand Package

Once you have achieved Maximum Medical Improvement (MMI), it's time to gather your documentation and other resources and have your legal team prepare a thorough demand package.

The demand package is an extensive document, with supporting materials, that is provided to the insurance company. It's the official demand for settlement of your case. Typically, your attorney will include standard components. As a claimant and as a good client, your job is to provide information, documentation, ideas and energy to your legal team so that together you can develop and present a complete picture of how your life has changed.

Theme

This is usually a short paragraph that introduces the demand package. The theme sells your case to the insurance company. It personalizes your experience and portrays you as a likeable person living a good life until tragedy struck.

Ms. Grazetti is a 26 year old woman who has spent her life preparing for a career in ballet. Since the collision, she has been unable to continue to dance professionally and lost her role in a Broadway play. She has discontinued training with a world renowned performing artist and moved out of her New York apartment. She started a new career and is struggling as a real estate agent in Tukwila. She was forced to move back home with her parents to make ends meet.

The theme of a demand package grabs the reader's attention and provides a real, human perspective to the damage and loss caused by the collision.

Collision Summary

This section summarizes the facts of the collision, including date, time, location and participants. A description of how the collision occurred includes the resulting property damage and any law enforcement action. More importantly it describes the dynamics of how the bodies were whipped, tossed and thrown about within the vehicle. We refer to this as the biomechanics of the collision. Explaining and proving how the injuries occurred is sometimes as important as detailing the nature and extent of the injuries. It is in this section that we attempt to convey the "wince effect". The reader should feel the pain and subconsciously agree that someone really got hurt. This is done using a combination of persuasive techniques, including photographs, animated computer graphics, engineer's calculations, re-creations, sample tests and national research data. In cases of disputed liability, eye witness, police and expert testimony is combined.

Injuries and Medical Treatment

In this section, the nature and extent of the injuries are detailed, including a chronology of the medical treatment. Special attention is given to addressing the need for that care and the reasonableness of the charges. The degree of temporary and/or permanent impairment is clearly stated and backed with indisputable proof, along with discussions regarding the implications that occurred because of permanent injuries. Here extensive reference to the theme is made, detailing how the injuries adversely affected the quality of life, at work and home.

Most everyone's self esteem is guided by what they do. If a person can't do what they love because of a collision, they have suffered a traumatic loss. Identifying the loss or losses and developing a narrative around that theme are key elements in persuasion. This becomes the draft script for opening remarks to a potential jury.

Charts are included in demand letters that separately summarize the medical bills and providers, with subtotals for each provider and a grand total for all medical care. Future wage loss or loss of earning capacity can be statistically calculated. Repeating the theme and supporting it visually with graphics, drawings, photographs, time lines and PowerPoint presentations all combine to making the demand more powerful.

Out-of-Pocket Expenses

All past and future out-of-pocket expenses, including mileage to and from your health care providers, are included. The list of expenses should punctuate the theme again. Not every cost is mentioned, instead we highlight those that dovetail with how the injuries have altered the injured person's lifestyle. A table displaying itemized expenses and a grand total is an effective method for communicating this information. Blending this with more narrative humanizes the story. One of the goals is to get the insurance company to say: "We don't want this case in front of a jury." Insurance companies identify which cases to take to trial and rarely is that the goal of the injured or his legal team.

Future Losses

Future economic losses are also figured and summarized in a table. Future medical bills, wage loss and out-of-pocket expenses are included. Medical providers provide probable estimates of anticipated future medical costs.

Arbitration

When negotiations stall, arbitration is frequently considered. What is it? Arbitration is a dispute resolution method that has grown increasingly popular as court calendars sag because of delays and escalating trial costs. Arbitration is a quick and efficient way to resolve claims without the cost, delay and exhaustive hassles of courtroom litigation. Courts and private groups offer arbitration services.

When your legal team agrees to go into arbitration, you participate in the selection of the arbitrator. A professional arbitrator generally has extensive experience in injury law. An arbitrator may be a retired judge or a practicing attorney. The arbitrator will listen to your side and the insurance company's side in an informal, relaxed setting. The arbitrator conducts discussions with both parties to gain an understanding of the issues and circumstances involved in the case. It is the arbitrator's job to act as an objective, unbiased intermediary during these discussions.

The attorney and the insurance company present their cases in the same room on the same day. Both sides have an opportunity to argue their case at the close to the arbitrator. The arbitrator then independently reviews and evaluates the merits of the case and weighs the evidence and testimony. He or she will ultimately determine liability and an amount to award as damages.

Arbitration is similar to a trial in that all of the facts of the case are presented to the arbitrator who then acts as "judge" and "jury" and decides the outcome of the case. The big differences are that arbitration is less costly, requires less preparation, is more expedient and produces substantially less stress than a trial. Many insurance companies are responsive to a demand for arbitration, because it means lower legal costs.

An arbitrator will often grant an award that falls somewhere between the insurance company's most recent offer and your most recent demand. Arbitration is not the environment where large, dramatic sums are awarded. The public court systems have a cap on the amount an arbitrator can award. This is a non-threatening process that may be the best place to resolve stalled negotiations.

> If you find that your settlement negotiations aren't getting anywhere, and especially if the insurance company's offer is significantly lower than your demand, you may want to consider arbitration. This is an excellent environment for neutral and reasoned discussion and resolution of claims.

When the parties involved in a dispute undertake to arbitrate a matter, they may agree beforehand if the arbitrator's final decision will be binding or non-binding. If the decision is binding, the participants in the arbitration may not petition the court to change the decision after the proceedings have concluded. However, if the decision is not binding, the parties involved may turn to the courts if they are dissatisfied with the outcome of arbitration.

Mediation

Mediation is an alternative to arbitration. It is attractive to parties sitting on opposite sides of a dispute. Mediation charges are reasonable, and the bill is shared equally by the parties.

Mediation is not based on the relative merits of the case. This means that the attorney will not be going into the details of the case with the mediator, nor will the insurance company. In mediation, it's assumed that the history of the case has already been discussed and understood by the parties. The facts, claims or beliefs of either side are not relevant during mediation. The mediator is primarily concerned with bringing the respective parties to a point of agreement on the dollar amount of the settlement. Mediation is a streamlined exercise to bring the dispute to a financial resolution. The decision to resolve the matter is left to the parties, not in the hands of a third party, like an arbitrator or jury.

Mediation is usually conducted at the mediator's office. There the parties are separated into different rooms. Mediations take either a half or full day. The mediator goes back and forth between the rooms. The injured person is not confronted by the defense attorney or cross-examined. The injured person is not expected to testify or sit in the witness chair. The setting is even more casual and comfortable than an arbitration. It is, however, taken seriously and conducted professionally.

The mediator will ask the insurance company for its highest possible settlement offer and will ask the injured claimant for the lowest acceptable dollar amount. Without disclosing the other party's "bottom line," the mediator then proceeds to work with both parties to discover what it will take to bring the parties to a common figure.

For example, you're asking for $20,000 compensation for your injuries, pain and suffering. You refuse to take any less, because you're still going to your Chiropractor for pain relief and you're concerned that your medical care will continue beyond any settlement date. The insurance company solidly refuses to offer more than $12,000, because your medical care to date totals $5,400 and they really don't think you'll need additional medical care. The two of you have been going around for months on these figures, but are hopelessly stalled.

The mediator will note the respective dollar amounts and begin discussions with both sides to reach a compromise. The mediator may be able to get the insurance company to come up to $17,000 and provide a guarantee that they'll pick up whatever reasonable and related medical costs you incur over the next three years. The mediator may also be able to convince your first-party carrier to take less on their subrogation demand. This is an acceptable compromise to you and the insurance companies. It calms your fears about future medical costs and puts more cash in your pocket.

> **Mediation is very much an exercise in compromise. Professional mediators are highly skilled at getting opposing parties to disengage from stubborn adherence to "win or lose" and focus instead on a "win/win" approach to conflict resolution. Mediation is *not* binding. Therefore, either party to mediation may turn to the courts if the matter does not settle.**

The insurance company is happy because it doesn't have to pony up much more cash than it was willing to pay coming into mediation. It allows the company to rely on its belief that your particular injuries won't require extensive additional medical treatment. It's a good compromise.

Mediation is an excellent alternative to protracted settlement negotiations and costly litigation. It avoids the physical, emotional and psychological stress and strain of continued litigation. Many claimants and their attorneys choose mediation because of the increased likelihood of a reasonable resolution of the claim without having to rehash all of the painful details and exhaustive proof. Mediation is advantageous because it allows the involved parties, not an outsider such as a judge, to determine the outcome of a claim.

With mediation, the parties to a conflict are brought together by the appointed mediator to identify and address those issues targeted for compromise. Mediation is non-confrontational by nature. It requires the full cooperation and participation of all parties to successfully reach an accord that is fair and acceptable. Mediation is a mutually cooperative and a constructive alternative for conflict resolution. It identifies and rectifies problems without causing additional damages or stresses to the participants.

Litigation

Sometimes, certain aspects of a claim may make an early insurance settlement unlikely or unwise and may preclude the possibility of arbitration. The insurance industry regularly reviews claims. If yours falls into one of a number of categories, your claim may automatically be headed for full-blown litigation before a judge and jury.

In this situation, because of circumstances completely beyond your control, there is nothing you can do to avoid litigation. No matter how diligently, reasonably and responsibly your legal team has tried to settle your case, the insurance company continues to refuse to settle. They'll insist on litigating your case before a judge and jury.

If you sense that your case is going to be litigated, understand that under no circumstance should you proceed without the best legal representation. Because of packed court calendars you should hire an attorney early in the process. Trial dates can be two years away. The sooner you partner with a legal team, the quicker you'll achieve full recovery.

Litigation Indicators

There are some indicators that an insurance company will vigorously look for and recognize when deciding if your case should be litigated. If your situation reflects any of these, seek immediate assistance from an attorney.

1. **Liability is contested.** You say it's his fault, and he says you're the one who caused the collision. Even worse, the police report is unclear as to who caused the collision.

2. **Multiple parties are involved.** You were struck by a pick-up, careen off an oncoming Volvo, take out a parked station wagon and land upside down in a ditch. It gets even more complicated if other parties to the collision were injured.

3. **There is another contributing cause.** Was the road poorly designed? Did a construction crew leave debris in the middle of your lane? Did a child rush into the street, causing the car in front of you to swerve and slam on the brakes? Any time something other than your own driving caused your property damage and injury, the insurance company will likely look to other potential sources of financial remuneration for your claim. As additional parties are brought into your insurance claim, and more people become concerned with passing the financial burden onto someone else, the chances of your case making it all the way to litigation increase dramatically.

4. **Vehicle damage is low.** This is a red alert for insurance companies! They're looking for the minor fender bender that produces a $10,000 injury claim. Certainly minor impacts can cause serious injuries. But unfortunately, some unscrupulous claimants have tried to get unreasonable settlements following such collisions. They've alerted the insurance industry to potential fraud in situations where minor property damage did not actually cause serious injuries.

5. **Significant injuries.** If you were seriously injured in an accident, or if your injuries were permanent or disabling, the financial value of your claim increases. So too does the insurance company's desire to keep its money in its own bank accounts. The cost of litigation may well be worth the expense to an insurance company intent on not paying out a large settlement claim. This is a sure sign that litigation is forthcoming.

6. **Multiple collisions.** If you have a history of multiple collisions before the one now, your claim becomes more complicated. The insurance company may raise concerns that you're an irresponsible or dangerous driver, that you're purposefully staging the collision to claim insurance money or that some of your present claims for property damage or injury result from earlier collisions.

7. **Pre-existing conditions.** The validity of your claims becomes muddied by the existence of old injuries, especially if they increase the pain or disability that you are presently claiming. Insurance companies are not eager to provide payments for old problems. It is your responsibility to prove, more likely than not, that your pain and suffering were caused by the injuries received in this collision.

8. **Gaps in treatment.** If you didn't seek medical help immediately after the collision, or if you have long periods of time during which you didn't receive any medical care, the insurance company will question the seriousness of your claim and will fight tooth and nail before paying you a dime.

9. **Anything that looks like fraud.** Be truthful! Make reasonable and ethical demands. Just one little slip-up and you'll find yourself in the courtroom facing a judge and jury who may be easily convinced that there's something fishy about your claim. They'll likely not believe any point of your case.

10. **The injured person doesn't present well.** It's a fact: if the jury doesn't like you as a person, you're probably not going to win. An abrasive personality, lack of good personal grooming, open hostility or a phony presentation may convince the jury, without any help from the opposing side, that you don't deserve to win.

11. **The insurance company can detect a sense of urgency or desperation to settle.** The insurance company is going to wonder, "What's the hurry here? What is this claimant afraid we'll discover?" They'll likely do everything in their power to stall your claim all the way to the courthouse steps. If the insurance company senses that you're on the defensive, watch out!

12. **The plaintiff is pro se, which means the Plaintiff represents himself/herself.** The average person simply cannot compete with an experienced insurance litigator and the deep financial pockets of the insurance industry and mount a successful litigation offense.

13. **Excessive medical bills.** If your medical bills and expenses are disproportionately high relative to the nature of your injuries, you'd better be prepared to accept a settlement amount that is less than the actual medical costs you incurred. Otherwise, the insurance company will take you to court. It won't be difficult for them to prove that you don't deserve compensation for what they will depict as unreasonable and unnecessary medical costs.

14. **An insurance company that is more likely to litigate.** There's no way to predict when this might happen, because the list of insurance companies that are more likely to litigate changes over time. Remain aware throughout your settlement negotiations of the willingness of the insurance company to settle. If they're acting like hard-liners, then they probably are hard-liners, and will

likely take you to court rather than ruin their coveted record of always settling low or not at all.

15. **Self-employed with a large wage loss claim.** It's very difficult to accurately prove lost wages when you're self-employed. Insurance companies love to take full advantage of this fact. If you're self-employed, realize that settlement is going to be tough. Unless you're willing to compromise or obtain professional legal help early on, you will end up in court.

16. **The injured person has unrealistic expectations as to the value of the claim.** Everyone wants full and reasonable compensation for property damage, injuries and pain and suffering. Just what qualifies as "full" or "reasonable" is open to interpretation, depending on whose side you're on. But if you still haven't reached an acceptable compromise after diligent settlement negotiations with the insurance company, consider the possibility that you may be off base in your expectations. If you're asking too much, the insurance company will simply refuse to move closer to your demand. Listen to your legal team. Trust their experience, judgment and advice.

If any of these litigation indicators apply to your case, a word to the wise: hire an experienced personal injury attorney immediately. Let his office handle all of the extremely demanding requirements and front the high costs of litigation.

Trial lawyers spend years and years learning how to best present a case and win it before a judge and jury. It is well beyond the scope of this book to provide you with an introduction to trial litigation. If your case is headed to a judge and jury, you will be doing yourself a tremendous disfavor if you opt to represent yourself in court.

Summary

The most important aspect of a successful recovery and resolution is preparation. Preparation means understanding the process. Preparation means assisting your legal team by being regularly involved but not getting in the way. Preparation starts the first day you hire an attorney with clear, consistent communications. Preparation also means being helpful in the management of your bills, records and other supporting documentation that establishes indisputable proof of your injuries and damages. Most folks find that they can manage their physical recovery side, but are happy to leave the paperwork up to their legal team. Paperwork requires administrative and organizational skills and no small amount of time, energy and effort to marshal the documentation.

Remember, negotiation is a process. Negotiation is a compromise. It's the gray area between what you want and what the insurance company is willing to pay. Believe it or not, negotiation can even be fun if you've got the right frame of mind. If you approach negotiation as a black and white battle of win or lose, right or wrong, no matter how much you come away with in settlement, you're likely to walk away with a bad experience. Learn to trust and work with your legal team. They are your partners. Listen, and make sure they listen to you. Speak up when necessary. Offer to grab an oar and pull.

Everything gets resolved, one way or the other. We've explained a few alternatives, arbitration and mediation, and reviewed an alternative that we don't recommend, courtroom litigation. Those trial indicators should be taken seriously. If you answered yes to one or more, hire the best injury attorney you can find immediately. While the system of courtroom justice in our country is in many respects the envy of the world, it can be a confusing, frustrating and heavily congested avenue to conflict resolution. If your case is headed for court you will need an experienced warrior on your side in battle. Jury trials are unpredictable. Your odds improve with a team that spends their professional lives fighting large insurance companies in that arena.

No matter how you decide to pursue your claim, whether on your own or with the best personal injury attorney you can hire, focus on getting better physically, mentally and emotionally. Make your first priority returning to 100%.

You'll make the entire experience less stressful and far more successful if you remember that this isn't a "win or lose" proposition. Keep your sense of humor, follow the guidelines presented in this book and know when to ask for help.

If you still have questions, call any one of my offices for a free consultation. We're in your neighborhood. We are passionate about what we do, and we only battle insurance companies on behalf of the injured. We solve problems. We are one of the largest and most successful injury law firms in Washington.

Survival Guide 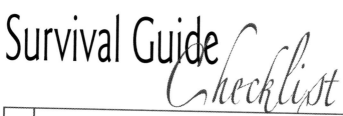 Checklist

✓	*Strategies Attorneys Use To Resolve Cases*
	Assist in the collection of all records, bills and photos. Participate in the preparation of witness statements and expert reports.
	Hire the best P.I. attorney you can find if your claim is too large for you to handle effectively.
	Work closely with your legal team in developing your demand package. Communicate often and clearly.
	Know the litigation indicators that will send your case to court.
	Keep your sense of humor.
	Make your physical recovery your top priority. Let your legal team stress about the details.
	Appreciate that settlement is a compromise.

A

Advance, Simple 103

Advance, with Interest 104

Alternatives to Settlement . . . . 161, 178 - 187

Arbitration . . . . 178 - 179

Attitude . . . . *See Temperament*

Attorney . . . . *See Representation*

Authorization to Release 74

B

Bad faith 4

Billing Directly by Attorney 104

Billing Monthly by Attorney 104

Bills

    automobile repair . . . . 6 - 8

    management by attorney 79

    marshaling 162, 171

    paid by PIP . . . . 46 - 51

    payment . . . . 38 - 40

    submitting . . . . 38 - 40

Business insurance . . . . . *See Insurance coverages: Business Related*

A 32 Year History of Helping People

C

Checklists

    Attorney Communications 106

    Attorney Qualifications 96

    Attorney Referral 87

    Demand Package 164, 175

    Depression 142

    Health Care Provider Communications 119

    PIP Benefits 52

    Policy Review 30

    Quality Of Life 153

    Quality Of Work 151

    Wage Loss 147

Chiropractic . . . . 25, 46, 113, 124 - 125

Colossus . . . . 165 - 166, 168

Communication

    with attorney . . . . 106 - 107

    with medical care team 61

Contingency Fee . . . . 101 - 102

Costs

    incurred by attorney 103

    litigation 184

Credit Disability Insurance 28

D

Demand Letter 177

Demand Package 164, 175

Depression . . . . .122, 140 - 143, 152

    warning signs 142

Diary 63

Diminution in value 14

Documentation

    effects of injury on employment . . . . 156 - 158, 174 - 175

    effects of injury on lifestyle . . . . .136 - 143

    needed for self-representation . . . . . 58 - 59, 65 - 66, 68 - 69

    of property damage 15, 176, 184

E

Emergency Room 112, 124, 162

Employment . . . . *See Self-employment*

Eyewitness accounts, gathering 62

North Puget Sound Neighborhood Offices

F

Fair market value 5, 12, 14, 16

Fee Agreement with Attorney .99 - 101

Finding Medical Care . . . . .111 - 117

Follow Up Care . . . . .61, 112 - 113, 121

Full coverage 22

G

Good faith 4, 6, 36, 171

Graham, John . . . .(800) 422-4610

H

Head and Brain Injury

    effect on lifestyle . . . . .138 - 140

Health insurance 27, 34, 37, 45

Help - Toll Free Number . . . .(800) 422-4610

Holistic Care. . . . . .126 - 127

Homeowner's insurance 27

I

I.M.E., Independent Medical Examination 75

Initial Consultation with Attorney . . . . .90 - 93

Insurance

  asking the right questions 22

  company slow to pay . . . . 33 - 34

  coverages 21

    Business 27

    Credit Disability 28

    Health 53, 102, 126, 163

    Homeowner's 27

    Liability 26

    Mortgage Disability 28

    PIP, Personal Injury Protection . . . . 25, 43 - 55

    UIM, Underinsured Motorist . . . . 22, 25 - 26

    UM, Uninsured Motorist . . . . 25 - 26

  evaluating policies . . . . 22 - 24, 30 - 32

  first-party carrier 37, 48, 181

  full coverage 22

  identifying policies 24

  injury coverage . . . . 31 - 32

  no coverage . . . . 26, 73 - 74

  reimbursement to first-party carrier . . . . 36 - 40

  stacking policies . . . . 32 - 33

  third-party carrier . . . . 47 - 48, 51, 53 - 54

  where to begin . . . . 22 - 23

Insurance Carriers

  out of state 76, 88

  treating pro se claimants 59, 69

South Puget Sound Neighborhood Offices

J

John Graham . . . . (800) 422-4610

Judges & Court Personnel

    treating pro se claimants 59, 69

K

Key players, negotiating with 35, 41

L

Liability . . . . 34 - 35, 183

    determining . . . . 41, 44 - 45

    insurance coverage 176, 178

Lifestyle changes 163

    depression . . . . 122, 140 - 143, 152

    documenting effects of injury on employment . . . . . 144 - 152

    head and brain injury . . . . 79, 122, 139 - 140

    physical injury 140, 142

    proof of damages 145, 147, 187

    quality of life . . . . 152 - 153, 165, 176

    self-employment . . . . 145 - 147

Litigation . . . . 86 - 87, 178, 182 - 189

    costs 184

    indicators 183

GLPattorneys.com

M

Managing Medical Records . . . . .120 - 121

Managing Multiple Caregivers 122

Managing Recovery . . . . .117 - 118

Mediation . . . . .180 - 182, 187, 189

Medical Care

    alternative 124

    Chiropractic .25, 46, 113, 124 - 125

    emergency room 112, 124, 162

    follow-up 113

    patient behavior . . . . .130 - 131

    shopping for . . . . .116 - 117

    traditional . . . . .124 - 125

Medical care team 61

    communication with . . . . .118 - 119

    management by attorney 111, 123

    managing multiple caregivers 122

    treating pro se claimants 69

Mitigating damages 5

MMI, Maximum Medical Improvement . . . . .127 - 129

Mortgage Disability 28

GRAHAM LUNDBERG & PESCHEL

N

Negotiation

strategy 53, 55

with key players . . . . .35 - 36

P

Patient Behavior . . . . .130 - 131

Payment, for bills . . . . .38 - 40

Personal belongings, removal from vehicle 5

Physical Injury, effect on lifestyle . . . . 137 - 138, 152 - 157

PIP, Personal Injury Protection . . . . .43 - 55

benefits paid . . . . .46 - 47

coverage . . . . .44 - 45

defined 44

Pocketing the money, for vehicle repair 8

Pre-existing Medical Condition 77

Pro Se Claimant . . . . *See Representation by Self*

defined 59

treatment by the "system" . . . . .69 - 71

insurance carriers 70

judges & court personnel 71

medical providers 69

Proof of Damages . . . . .15 - 16

Property Damage, minimal . . . . .76 - 77, 184

CRASHCOURSE101.COM

Q

Quality of Life . . . . .128, 152 - 153, 165, 176

Questions . . . .(800) 422-4610

R

Recorded Statement 74, 157

Records

    management . . . . .79, 120 - 121

    marshaling 162, 171

Recovery

    Maximum Medical Improvement . . . . .127 - 129

    physical difficulties . . . . .114 - 116

    managing . . . . .117 - 118

Referral, attorney sources 87

Reimbursement to first-party carrier . . . . 36 - 37, 181 - 182

Rental car . . . . .3, 11 - 12, 22, 62

Repairs

    choice of shop . . . . 3 - 7, 11 - 12, 14

    cost exceeds value of vehicle . . . . *See Total Loss*

    negotiating who pays . . . . .2 - 3

    of personal items 10

    parts used . . . . .8 - 9

    payment for 7

    taking delivery of repaired vehicle 9

John Graham, Attorney at Law

Representation

   By an Attorney

      advance, simple 103

      advance with interest 104

      benefits . . . . .86 - 88

      billing directly 104

      billing monthly 104

      contingency fee . . . . .101 - 102

      costs 103

      determining if needed . . . . 57 - 58, 72 - 78

      fee agreement . . . . .99 - 101

      first phone call 88

      initial consultation . . . . .23, 72, 90 - 91

      managing bills 79

      managing medical care .78 - 80

      personal injury specialists . . . . .86 - 88

      qualifying to handle case 95, 117

      referral sources . . . . .86 - 88

      retainer 104

      trial costs 105, 178

   By Self - qualifications to consider

      Time . . . . .60 - 64

      Temperament . . . . .64 - 67

      Talent . . . . .67 - 69

      treatment by the "system" . . . . .69 - 71

S

Self-Representation . . . . *See Pro Se Claimant*

Self-Employment, effects of injury . . . . .145 - 148

Settlement . . . . .161 - 174

    arbitration . . . . .178 - 179

    litigation . . . . .183 - 187

    mediation . . . . .180 - 182

   demand letter 177

   demand package presentation . . . . .175 - 177

Signing, authorization to release 74

Stacking . . . . .32 - 33

Storage, of vehicle . . . . .2 - 6

Submitting bills . . . . .38 - 40

T

Talent . . . . 58 - 59, 67 - 69, 72, 83

    questioned . . . . .68 - 69

Telephone, use in self-representation. 61

Temperament . . . . 58 - 59, 64 - 68, 72, 83

    changes in . . . . .65 - 66

Time, required for

   self representation 60

   communications with employer 62

   daily diary 63

We Teach Doctors About Insurance

    documentation 62

    eyewitness accounts 62

    medical team 61

    telephone 61

    transportation 62

Total loss . . . . 12 - 13

Towing . . . . 2 - 4, 6 - 7, 13, 22, 61

Transportation 62

Trial costs 105, 178

U

Underinsured motorist (UIM) coverage . . . . 25 - 26, 31

Uninsured motorist (UM) coverage . . . . 25 - 26

V

Value

    determination 165

    diminution 14

    of personal items 10

    of vehicle before accident . . . . 12 - 13

W

Wage Loss

    documenting . . . . 147 - 148

    proving 147

Practice Limited to Injury Law

ACRONYMS

IME	Independent Medical Examination
MMI	Maximum Medical Improvement
MRI	Magnetic Resonance Imaging
PD	Property Damage
PI	Personal Injury
PIP	Personal Injury Protection
UM	Uninsured Motorist
UIM	Underinsured Motorist

Your Questions Answered

Injury Attorneys Since 1979

GRAHAM LUNDBERG & PESCHEL is one of the largest and best injury law firms in the State of Washington. GLP limits its practice to the handling of injury cases. For more than 32 years they have battled insurance companies. **GLP** has extensive experience in a wide variety of personal injury cases including:

- Motor Vehicle and Truck Collisions
- Pedestrian and Cycle Accidents
- Construction Site Injuries
- Workplace Injuries
- Unsafe Property
- Defective Products
- Maritime Injuries
- Wrongful Death

The attorneys at **GLP** are an experienced team, fully staffed to assist injured parties. Their teams are devoted and have the resources to guide clients through the complexities of each case. They provide free initial consultations to any prospective client, assess the issues in the case, determine if an attorney is needed and whether **GLP** is the right legal team for the particular needs of the client.

Their large teams have departments that obtain benefits which may include:

- Medical Expenses
- Lost Wages
- Loss of Future Earning Capacity
- Property Losses (Car and Truck Damage)
- Physical and Mental Pain and Suffering
- Impairment, Disability and Pensions

GRAHAM LUNDBERG & PESCHEL has multiple locations through out Washington with neighborhood offices. We offer next-day air service to our clients in central and eastern Washington. GLP fees are earned on a contingent fee basis plus costs. Attorney's fees are paid when the case is resolved with the insurance company. If there is no recovery, clients pay NO fee for the legal services only for the costs incurred.

GRAHAM LUNDBERG & PESCHEL recommends some tips for finding a competent team of attorneys and staff:

- Look for extensive experience.
- Only consider firms that limit their practice to injury law, any old lawyer won't do.
- Evaluate the success rate of the firm.
- Inquire about their effectiveness in dealing with insurance companies. There should be a good, verifiable track record of settling claims without resorting to litigation.
- Ask your physician about the firm's reputation. Has he worked with them? Would he refer his family to them?

GRAHAM LUNDBERG & PESCHEL's teams of attorneys, paralegals, legal assistants and entire staff are dedicated to providing professional advocacy, along with caring and supportive guidance in the area of personal injury law. They undertake all aspects of each case to alleviate the stress and frustration inevitably created by the claims process, leaving the client free to focus on their treatment and rehabilitation. GLP has multiple trial successes with large jury verdicts. GLP won at the Supreme Court in Washington against State Farm on significant insurance and injury law issues. That case took over 10 years. They are dedicated to fighting, fighting hard and winning! You'll like their style. You'll like their friendliness. They solve problems and they are in your neighborhood.

ABOUT THE AUTHOR

Attorney John M. Graham, B.A., B.S., J.D., is a renowned leader and speaker in the field of insurance law and serious injury settlements. John Graham is a graduate of Northwestern University, Oregon State University and the University of Puget Sound School of Law. He was admitted to practice in Washington State and the Federal Courts in 1979. He is the senior partner in GRAHAM LUNDBERG & PESCHEL, one of Washington's largest injury firms and one of the most successful. He is an energetic advocate for the injured.

One of John Graham's passions is writing and teaching. He has educated physicians and providers for more than 32 years and lectures regularly to students, attorneys and the injured. His teaching emphasizes the legal and insurance aspects of injury law. Crash Course 101, is in its 6th edition with over 85,000 copies in print.

John is an avid athlete, competing in marathons and triathlons. He is an instructor in martial arts and has surfed exotic hidden locations. He resides in Kirkland with his wife and kids. They have traveled extensively, including a two year trip circumnavigating the world. John has climbed Mount Kilimanjaro (19,340') and Mount Rainier (14,411').

John believes in the team approach to handling serious injury cases. He has built one of the best, if not the best, injury team of professionals available. His team's successes and results are lengthy and remarkable. You'll like his style. You'll like his team. Crash Course 101 reveals his strategies for negotiating with insurance companies. His proven methods have helped thousands of injured people decrease their stress and increase their settlement dollars. Now you can be of assistance to your legal team and better achieve full physical and financial recovery after an accident.